A COURSE IN MIRACLES

MANUAL FOR TEACHERS

FOUNDATION FOR INNER PEACE

Published by
Foundation for Inner Peace
P.O. Box 635
Tiburon, CA 94920

Second Printing – June 1977

Third Printing – October 1977

Fourth Printing – January 1978

Fifth Printing – September 1978

Sixth Printing – October 1979

Seventh Printing – September 1980

Eighth Printing – December 1980

Ninth Printing – September 1981

Tenth Printing – May 1982

Eleventh Printing – February 1983

Twelfth Printing – February 1984

Thirteenth Printing—September 1984

MANUAL FOR TEACHERS

CONTENTS

CLARIFICATION OF TERMS

CONTENTS

MANUAL FOR TEACHERS

INTRODUCTION

The role of teaching and learning is actually reversed in the thinking of the world. The reversal is characteristic. It seems as if the teacher and the learner are separated, the teacher giving something to the learner rather than to himself. Further, the act of teaching is regarded as a special activity, in which one engages only a relatively small proportion of one's time. The course, on the other hand, emphasizes that to teach *is* to learn, so that teacher and learner are the same. It also emphasizes that teaching is a constant process; it goes on every moment of the day, and continues into sleeping thoughts as well.

To teach is to demonstrate. There are only two thought systems, and you demonstrate that you believe one or the other is true all the time. From your demonstration others learn, and so do you. The question is not whether you will teach, for in that there is no choice. The purpose of the course might be said to provide you with a means of choosing what you want to teach on the basis of what you want to learn. You cannot give to someone else, but only to yourself, and this you learn through teaching. Teaching is but a call to witnesses to attest to what you believe. It is a method of conversion. This is not done by words alone. Any situation must be to you a chance to teach others what you are, and what they are to you. No more than that, but also never less.

The curriculum you set up is therefore determined exclusively by what you think you are, and what you believe the relationship of others is to you. In the formal teaching situation, these questions may be totally unrelated to what you think you are teaching. Yet it is impossible not to use the content of any situation on behalf of what you really teach, and therefore really learn. To this the verbal content of your teaching is quite irrelevant. It may coincide with it, or it may not. It is the teaching underlying what you say that teaches you. Teaching but reinforces what you believe about yourself. Its fundamental purpose is to diminish self doubt. This does not mean that the self you are trying to protect is real. But it does mean that the self you think is real is what you teach.

This is inevitable. There is no escape from it. How could it be otherwise? Everyone who follows the world's curriculum, and everyone here does follow it until he changes his mind, teaches solely to convince himself that he is what he is not. Herein is the purpose of the world. What else, then, would its curriculum be? Into this hopeless and closed learning situation, which teaches nothing but despair and death, God sends His teachers. And as they teach His lessons of joy and hope, their learning finally becomes complete.

Except for God's teachers there would be little hope of salvation, for the world of sin would seem forever real. The self-deceiving must deceive, for they must teach deception. And what else is hell? This is a manual for the teachers of God. They are not perfect, or they would not be here. Yet it is their mission to become perfect here, and so they teach perfection over and over, in many, many ways, until they have learned it. And then they are seen no more, although their thoughts remain a source of strength and truth forever. Who are they? How are they chosen? What do they do? How can they work out their own salvation and the salvation of the world? This manual attempts to answer these questions.

WHO ARE GOD'S TEACHERS?

A teacher of God is anyone who chooses to be one. His qualifications consist solely in this; somehow, somewhere he has made a deliberate choice in which he did not see his interests as apart from someone else's. Once he has done that, his road is established and his direction is sure. A light has entered the darkness. It may be a single light, but that is enough. He has entered an agreement with God even if he does not yet believe in Him. He has become a bringer of salvation. He has become a teacher of God.

They come from all over the world. They come from all religions and from no religion. They are the ones who have answered. The Call is universal. It goes on all the time everywhere. It calls for teachers to speak for It and redeem the world. Many hear It, but few will answer. Yet it is all a matter of time. Everyone will answer in the end, but the end can be a long, long way off. It is because of this that the plan of the teachers was established. Their function is to save time. Each one begins as a single light, but with the Call at its center it is a light that cannot be limited. And each one saves a thousand years of time as the world judges it. To the Call Itself time has no meaning.

There is a course for every teacher of God. The form of the course varies greatly. So do the particular teaching aids involved. But the content of the course never changes. Its central theme is always, "God's Son is guiltless, and in his innocence is his salvation." It can be taught by actions or thoughts; in words or soundlessly; in any language or in no language; in any place or time or manner. It does not matter who the teacher was before he heard the Call. He has become a savior by his answering. He has seen someone else as himself. He has therefore found his own salvation and the salvation of the world. In his rebirth is the world reborn.

This is a manual for a special curriculum, intended for teachers of a special form of the universal course. There are many thousands of other forms, all with the same outcome. They merely save time. Yet it is time alone that winds on wearily, and the world is very tired now. It is old and worn and without hope. There was never a question of outcome, for what can change the Will of God? But time, with its illusions of change and death, wears out the world and all things in it. Yet time has an ending, and it is this that the teachers of God are appointed to bring about. For time is in their hands. Such was their choice, and it is given them.

WHO ARE THEIR PUPILS?

Certain pupils have been assigned to each of God's teachers, and they will begin to look for him as soon as he has answered the Call. They were chosen for him because the form of the universal curriculum that he will teach is best for them in view of their level of understanding. His pupils have been waiting for him, for his coming is certain. Again, it is only a matter of time. Once he has chosen to fulfill his role, they are ready to fulfill theirs. Time waits on his choice, but not on whom he will serve. When he is ready to learn, the opportunities to teach will be provided for him.

In order to understand the teaching-learning plan of salvation, it is necessary to grasp the concept of time that the course sets forth. Atonement corrects illusions, not truth. Therefore, it corrects what never was. Further, the plan for this correction was established and completed simultaneously, for the Will of God is entirely apart from time. So is all reality, being of Him. The instant the idea of separation entered the mind of God's Son, in that same instant was God's Answer given. In time this happened very long ago. In reality it never happened at all.

The world of time is the world of illusion. What happened long ago seems to be happening now. Choices made long since appear to be open; yet to be made. What has been learned and understood and long ago passed by is looked upon as a new thought, a fresh idea, a different approach. Because your will is free you can accept what has already happened at any time you choose, and only then will you realize that it was always there. As the course emphasizes, you are not free to choose the curriculum, or even the form in which you will learn it. You are free, however, to decide when you want to learn it. And as you accept it, it is already learned.

Time really, then, goes backward to an instant so ancient that it is beyond all memory, and past even the possibility of remembering. Yet because it is an instant that is relived again and again and still again, it seems to be now. And thus it is that pupil and teacher seem to come together in the present, finding each other as if they had not met before. The pupil comes at the right time to the right place. This is inevitable, because he made the right choice in that ancient instant which he now relives. So has the teacher, too, made an inevitable choice out of an ancient past. God's Will in everything but seems to take time in the working-out. What could delay the power of eternity?

When pupil and teacher come together, a teaching-learning situation begins. For the teacher is not really the one who does the teaching. God's Teacher speaks to any two who join together for learning purposes. The relationship is holy because of that purpose, and God has promised to send His Spirit into any holy relationship. In the teaching-learning situation, each one learns that giving and receiving are the same. The demarcations they have drawn between their roles, their minds, their bodies, their needs, their interests, and all the differences they thought separated them from one another, fade and grow dim and disappear. Those who would learn the same course share one interest and one goal. And thus he who was the learner becomes a teacher of God himself, for he has made the one decision that gave his teacher to him. He has seen in another person the same interests as his own.

The teachers of God have no set teaching level. Each teaching-learning situation involves a different relationship at the beginning, although the ultimate goal is always the same; to make of the relationship a holy relationship, in which both can look upon the Son of God as sinless. There is no one from whom a teacher of God cannot learn, so there is no one whom he cannot teach. However, from a practical point of view he cannot meet everyone, nor can everyone find him. Therefore, the plan includes very specific contacts to be made for each teacher of God. There are no accidents in salvation. Those who are to meet will meet, because together they have the potential for a holy relationship. They are ready for each other.

The simplest level of teaching appears to be quite superficial. It consists of what seem to be very casual encounters; a "chance" meeting of two apparent strangers in an elevator, a child who is not looking where he is going running into an adult "by chance," two students "happening" to walk home together. These are not chance encounters. Each of them has the potential for becoming a teaching-learning situation. Perhaps the seeming strangers in the elevator will smile to one another; perhaps the adult will not scold the child for bumping into him; perhaps the students will become friends. Even at the level of the most casual encounter, it is possible for two people to lose sight of separate interests, if only for a moment. That moment will be enough. Salvation has come.

It is difficult to understand that levels of teaching the universal course is a concept as meaningless in reality as is time. The illusion of one permits the illusion of the other. In time, the teacher of God seems to begin to change his mind about the world with a single decision, and then learns more and more about the new direction as he teaches it. We have covered the illusion of time already, but the illusion of levels of teaching seems to be something different. Perhaps the best way to demonstrate that these levels cannot exist is simply to say that any level of the teaching-learning situation is part of God's plan for Atonement, and His plan can have no levels, being a reflection of His Will. Salvation is always ready and always there. God's teachers work at different levels, but the result is always the same.

Each teaching-learning situation is maximal in the sense that each person involved will learn the most that he can from the other person at that time. In this sense, and in this sense only, we can speak of levels of teaching. Using the term in this way, the second level of teaching is a more sustained relationship, in which, for a time, two people enter into a fairly intense teaching-learning situation and then appear to separate. As with the first level, these meetings are not accidental, nor is what appears to be the end of the relationship a real end. Again, each has learned the most he can at the time. Yet all who meet will someday meet again, for it is the destiny of all relationships to become holy. God is not mistaken in His Son.

The third level of teaching occurs in relationships which, once they are formed, are lifelong. These are teaching-learning situations in which each person is given a chosen learning partner who presents him with unlimited opportunities for learning. These relationships are generally few, because their existence implies that those involved have reached a stage simultaneously in which the teaching-learning balance is actually perfect. This does not mean that they necessarily recognize this; in fact, they generally do not. They may even be quite hostile to each other for some time, and perhaps for life. Yet should they decide to learn it, the perfect lesson is before them and can be learned. And if they decide to learn that lesson, they become the saviors of the teachers who falter and may even seem to fail. No teacher of God can fail to find the Help he needs.

WHAT ARE THE CHARACTERISTICS OF GOD'S TEACHERS?

The surface traits of God's teachers are not at all alike. They do not look alike to the body's eyes, they come from vastly different backgrounds, their experiences of the world vary greatly, and their superficial "personalities" are quite distinct. Nor, at the beginning stages of their functioning as teachers of God, have they as yet acquired the deeper characteristics that will establish them as what they are. God gives special gifts to His teachers, because they have a special role in His plan for Atonement. Their specialness is, of course, only temporary; set in time as a means of leading out of time. These special gifts, born in the holy relationship toward which the teaching-learning situation is geared, become characteristic of all teachers of God who have advanced in their own learning. In this respect they are all alike.

All differences among the Sons of God are temporary. Nevertheless, in time it can be said that the advanced teachers of God have the following characteristics:

1. Trust

This is the foundation on which their ability to fulfill their function rests. Perception is the result of learning. In fact, perception *is* learning, because cause and effect are never separated. The teachers of God have trust in the world, because they have learned it is not governed by the laws the world made up. It is governed by a Power That is *in* them but not *of* them. It is this Power That keeps all things safe. It is through this Power that the teachers of God look on a forgiven world.

When this Power has once been experienced, it is impossible to trust one's own petty strength again. Who would attempt to fly with the tiny wings of a sparrow when the mighty power of an eagle has been given him? And who would place his faith in the shabby offerings of the ego when the gifts of God are laid before him? What is it that induces them to make the shift?

Development of trust

First, they must go through what might be called "a period of undoing." This need not be painful, but it usually is so experienced. It seems as if things are being taken away, and it is rarely understood initially that their lack of value is merely being recognized. How can lack of value be perceived unless the perceiver is in a position where he must see things in a different light? He is not yet at a point at which he can make the shift entirely internally. And so the plan will sometimes call for changes in what seem to be external circumstances. These changes are always helpful. When the teacher of God has learned that much, he goes on to the second stage.

Next, the teacher of God must go through "a period of sorting out." This is always somewhat difficult because, having learned that the changes in his life are always helpful, he must now decide all things on the basis of whether they increase the helpfulness or hamper it. He will find that many, if not most of the things he valued before will merely hinder his ability to transfer what he has learned to new situations as they arise. Because he has valued what is really valueless, he will not generalize the lesson for fear of loss and sacrifice. It takes great learning to understand that all things, events, encounters and circumstances are helpful. It is only to the extent to which they are helpful that any degree of reality should be accorded them in this world of illusion. The word "value" can apply to nothing else.

The third stage through which the teacher of God must go can be called "a period of relinquishment." If this is interpreted as giving up the desirable, it will engender enormous conflict. Few teachers of God escape this distress entirely. There is, however, no point in sorting out the valuable from the valueless unless the next obvious step is taken. Therefore, the period of overlap is apt to be one in which the teacher of God feels called upon to sacrifice his own best interests on behalf of truth. He has not realized as yet how wholly impossible such a demand would be. He can learn this only as he actually does give up the valueless. Through this, he learns that where he anticipated grief, he finds a happy lightheartedness instead; where he thought something was asked of him, he finds a gift bestowed on him.

Now comes "a period of settling down." This is a quiet time, in which the teacher of God rests a while in reasonable peace. Now he consolidates his learning. Now he begins to see the transfer value of what he has learned. Its potential is literally staggering, and the teacher of God is now at the point in his progress at which he sees in it his whole way out. "Give up what you do not want, and keep what you do." How simple is the obvious! And how easy to do! The teacher of God needs this period of respite. He has not yet come as far as he thinks. Yet when he is ready to go on, he goes with mighty companions beside him. Now he rests a while, and gathers them before going on. He will not go on from here alone.

The next stage is indeed "a period of unsettling." Now must the teacher of God understand that he did not really know what was valuable and what was valueless. All that he really learned so far was that he did not want the valueless, and that he did want the valuable. Yet his own sorting out was meaningless in teaching him the difference. The idea of sacrifice, so central to his own thought system, had made it impossible for him to judge. He thought he learned willingness, but now he sees that he does not know what the willingness is for. And now he must attain a state that may remain impossible to reach for a long, long time. He must learn to lay all judgment aside, and ask only what he really wants in every circumstance. Were not each step in this direction so heavily reinforced, it would be hard indeed!

And finally, there is "a period of achievement." It is here that learning is consolidated. Now what was seen as merely shadows before become solid gains, to be counted on in all "emergencies" as well as tranquil times. Indeed, the tranquility is their result; the outcome of honest learning, consistency of thought and full transfer. This is the stage of real peace, for here is Heaven's state fully reflected. From here, the way to Heaven is open and easy. In fact, it is here. Who would "go" anywhere, if peace of mind is already complete? And who would seek to change tranquility for something more desirable? What could be more desirable than this?

2. Honesty

All other traits of God's teachers rest on trust. Once that has been achieved, the others cannot fail to follow. Only the trusting can afford honesty, for only they can see its value. Honesty does not apply only to what you say. The term actually means consistency. There is nothing you say that contradicts what you think or do; no thought opposes any other thought; no act belies your word; and no word lacks agreement with another. Such are the truly honest. At no level are they in conflict with themselves. Therefore it is impossible for them to be in conflict with anyone or anything.

The peace of mind which the advanced teachers of God experience is largely due to their perfect honesty. It is only the wish to deceive that makes for war. No one at one with himself can even conceive of conflict. Conflict is the inevitable result of self deception, and self deception is dishonesty. There is no challenge to a teacher of God. Challenge implies doubt, and the trust on which God's teachers rest secure makes doubt impossible. Therefore they can only succeed. In this, as in all things, they are honest. They can only succeed, because they never do their will alone. They choose for all mankind; for all the world and all things in it; for the unchanging and unchangeable beyond appearances; and for the Son of God and his Creator. How could they not succeed? They choose in perfect honesty, sure of their choice as of themselves.

3. Tolerance

God's teachers do not judge. To judge is to be dishonest, for to judge is to assume a position you do not have. Judgment without self deception is impossible. Judgment implies that you have been deceived in your brothers. How, then, could you not have been deceived in yourself? Judgment implies a lack of trust, and trust remains the bedrock of the teacher of God's whole thought system. Let this be lost, and all his learning goes. Without judgment are all things equally acceptable, for who could judge otherwise? Without judgment are all men brothers, for who is there who stands apart? Judgment destroys honesty and shatters trust. No teacher of God can judge and hope to learn.

4. Gentleness

Harm is impossible for God's teachers. They can neither harm nor be harmed. Harm is the outcome of judgment. It is the dishonest act that follows a dishonest thought. It is a verdict of guilt upon a brother, and therefore on oneself. It is the end of peace and the denial of learning. It demonstrates the absence of God's curriculum, and its replacement by insanity. No teacher of God but must learn, —and fairly early in his training,—that harmfulness completely obliterates his function from his awareness. It will make him confused, fearful, angry and suspicious. It will make the Holy Spirit's lessons impossible to learn. Nor can God's Teacher be heard at all, except by those who realize that harm can actually achieve nothing. No gain can come of it.

Therefore, God's teachers are wholly gentle. They need the strength of gentleness, for it is in this that the function of salvation becomes easy. To those who would do harm, it is impossible. To those to whom harm has no meaning, it is merely natural. What choice but this has meaning to the sane? Who chooses hell when he perceives a way to Heaven? And who would choose the weakness that must come from harm in place of the unfailing, all-encompassing and limitless strength of gentleness? The might of God's teachers lies in their gentleness, for they have understood their evil thoughts came neither from God's Son nor his Creator. Thus did they join their thoughts with Him Who is their Source. And so their will, which always was His Own, is free to be itself.

5. Joy

Joy is the inevitable result of gentleness. Gentleness means that fear is now impossible, and what could come to interfere with joy? The open hands of gentleness are always filled. The gentle have no pain. They cannot suffer. Why would they not be joyous? They are sure they are beloved and must be safe. Joy goes with gentleness as surely as grief attends attack. God's teachers trust in Him. And they are sure His Teacher goes before them, making sure no harm can come to them. They hold His gifts and follow in His way, because God's Voice directs them in all things. Joy is their song of thanks. And Christ looks down on them in thanks as well. His need of them is just as great as theirs of Him. How joyous it is to share the purpose of salvation!

6. Defenselessness

God's teachers have learned how to be simple. They have no dreams that need defense against the truth. They do not try to make themselves. Their joy comes from their understanding Who created them. And does what God created need defense? No one can become an advanced teacher of God until he fully understands that defenses are but foolish guardians of mad illusions. The more grotesque the dream, the fiercer and more powerful its defenses seem to be. Yet when the teacher of God finally agrees to look past them, he finds that nothing was there. Slowly at first he lets himself be undeceived. But he learns faster as his trust increases. It is not danger that comes when defenses are laid down. It is safety. It is peace. It is joy. And it is God.

7. Generosity

The term generosity has special meaning to the teacher of God. It is not the usual meaning of the word; in fact, it is a meaning that must be learned and learned very carefully. Like all the other attributes of God's teachers this one rests ultimately on trust, for without trust no one can be generous in the true sense. To the world, generosity means "giving away" in the sense of "giving up." To the teachers of God, it means giving away in order to keep. This has been emphasized throughout the text and the workbook, but it is perhaps more alien to the thinking of the world than many other ideas in our curriculum. Its greater strangeness lies merely in the obviousness of its reversal of the world's thinking. In the clearest way possible, and at the simplest of levels, the word means the exact opposite to the teachers of God and to the world.

The teacher of God is generous out of self interest. This does not refer, however, to the self of which the world speaks. The teacher of God does not want anything he cannot give away, because he realizes it would be valueless to him by definition. What would he want it *for*? He could only lose because of it. He could not gain. Therefore he does not seek what only he could keep, because that is a guarantee of loss. He does not want to suffer. Why should he ensure himself pain? But he does want to keep for himself all things that are of God, and therefore for His Son. These are the things that belong to him. These he can give away in true generosity, protecting them forever for himself.

8. Patience

Those who are certain of the outcome can afford to wait, and wait without anxiety. Patience is natural to the teacher of God. All he sees is certain outcome, at a time perhaps unknown to him as yet, but not in doubt. The time will be as right as is the answer. And this is true for everything that happens now or in the future. The past as well held no mistakes; nothing that did not serve to benefit the world, as well as him to whom it seemed to happen. Perhaps it was not understood at the time. Even so, the teacher of God is willing to reconsider all his past decisions, if they are causing pain to anyone. Patience is natural to those who trust. Sure of the ultimate interpretation of all things in time, no outcome already seen or yet to come can cause them fear.

9. Faithfulness

The extent of the teacher of God's faithfulness is the measure of his advancement in the currriculum. Does he still select some aspects of his life to bring to his learning, while keeping others apart? If so, his advancement is limited, and his trust not yet firmly established. Faithfulness is the teacher of God's trust in the Word of God to set all things right; not some, but all. Generally, his faithfulness begins by resting on just some problems, remaining carefully limited for a time. To give up all problems to one Answer is to reverse the thinking of the world entirely. And that alone is faithfulness. Nothing but that really deserves the name. Yet each degree, however small, is worth achieving. Readiness, as the text notes, is not mastery.

True faithfulness, however, does not deviate. Being consistent, it is wholly honest. Being unswerving, it is full of trust. Being based on fearlessness, it is gentle. Being certain, it is joyous. And being confident, it is tolerant. Faithfulness, then, combines in itself the other attributes of God's teachers. It implies acceptance of the Word of God and His definition of His Son. It is to Them that faithfulness in the true sense is always directed. Toward Them it looks, seeking until it finds. And having found, it rests in quiet certainty on That alone to Which all faithfulness is due.

10. Open-Mindedness

The centrality of open-mindedness, perhaps the last of the attributes the teacher of God acquires, is easily understood when its relation to forgiveness is recognized. Open-mindedness comes with lack of judgment. As judgment shuts the mind against God's Teacher, so open-mindedness invites Him to come in. As condemnation judges the Son of God as evil, so open-mindedness permits him to be judged by the Voice for God on His behalf. As the projection of guilt upon him would send him to hell, so open-mindedness lets Christ's image be extended to him. Only the open-minded can be at peace, for they alone see reason for it.

How do the open-minded forgive? They have let go all things that would prevent forgiveness. They have in truth abandoned the world, and let it be restored to them in newness and in joy so glorious they could never have conceived of such a change. Nothing is now as it was formerly. Nothing but sparkles now which seemed so dull and lifeless before. And above all are all things welcoming, for threat is gone. No clouds remain to hide the face of Christ. Now is the goal achieved. Forgiveness is the final goal of the curriculum. It paves the way for what goes far beyond all learning. The curriculum makes no effort to exceed its legitimate goal. Forgiveness is its single aim, at which all learning ultimately converges. It is indeed enough.

You may have noticed that the list of attributes of God's teachers does not include things that are the Son of God's inheritance. Terms like love, sinlessness, perfection, knowledge and eternal truth do not appear in this context. They would be most inappropriate here. What God has given is so far beyond our curriculum that learning but disappears in its presence. Yet while its presence is obscured, the focus properly belongs on the curriculum. It is the function of God's teachers to bring true learning to the world. Properly speaking it is unlearning that they bring, for that is "true learning" in the world. It is given to the teachers of God to bring the glad tidings of complete forgiveness to the world. Blessed indeed are they, for they are the bringers of salvation.

HOW IS HEALING ACCOMPLISHED?

Healing involves an understanding of what the illusion of sickness is for. Healing is impossible without this.

1 The perceived purpose of sickness

Healing is accomplished the instant the sufferer no longer sees any value in pain. Who would choose suffering unless he thought it brought him something, and something of value to him? He must think it is a small price to pay for something of greater worth. For sickness is an election; a decision. It is the choice of weakness, in the mistaken conviction that it is strength. When this occurs, real strength is seen as threat and health as danger. Sickness is a method, conceived in madness, for placing God's Son on his Father's throne. God is seen as outside, fierce and powerful, eager to keep all power for Himself. Only by His death can He be conquered by His Son.

And what, in this insane conviction, does healing stand for? It symbolizes the defeat of God's Son and the triumph of his Father over him. It represents the ultimate defiance in a direct form which the Son of God is forced to recognize. It stands for all that he would hide from himself to protect his "life." If he is healed, he is responsible for his thoughts. And if he is responsible for his thoughts, he will be killed to prove to him how weak and pitiful he is. But if he chooses death himself, his weakness is his strength. Now has he given himself what God would give to him, and thus entirely usurped the throne of his Creator.

2. The shift in perception

Healing must occur in exact proportion to which the valuelessness of sickness is recognized. One need but say, "There is no gain at all to me in this" and he is healed. But to say this, one first must recognize certain facts. First, it is obvious that decisions are of the mind, not of the body. If sickness is but a faulty problem-solving approach, it is a decision. And if it is a decision, it is the mind and not the body that makes it. The resistance to recognizing this is enormous, because the existence of the world as you perceive it depends on the body being the decision-maker. Terms like "instincts," "reflexes" and the like represent attempts to endow the body with non-mental motivators. Actually, such terms merely state or describe the problem. They do not answer it.

The acceptance of sickness as a decision of the mind, for a purpose for which it would use the body, is the basis of healing. And this is so for healing in all forms. A patient decides that this is so, and he recovers. If he decides against recovery, he will not be healed. Who is the physician? Only the mind of the patient himself. The outcome is what he decides that it is. Special agents seem to be ministering to him, yet they but give form to his own choice. He chooses them in order to bring tangible form to his desires. And it is this they do, and nothing else. They are not actually needed at all. The patient could merely rise up without their aid and say, "I have no use for this." There is no form of sickness that would not be cured at once.

What is the single requisite for this shift in perception? It is simply this; the recognition that sickness is of the mind, and has nothing to do with the body. What does this recognition "cost"? It costs the whole world you see, for the world will never again appear to rule the mind. For with this recognition is responsibility placed where it belongs; not with the world, but on him who looks on the world and sees it as it is not. He looks on what he chooses to see. No more and no less. The world does nothing to him. He only thought it did. Nor does he do anything to the world, because he was mistaken about what it is. Herein is the release from guilt and sickness both, for they are one. Yet to accept this release, the insignificance of the body must be an acceptable idea.

With this idea is pain forever gone. But with this idea goes also all confusion about creation. Does not this follow of necessity? Place cause and effect in their true sequence in one respect, and the learning will generalize and transform the world. The transfer value of one true idea has no end or limit. The final outcome of this lesson is the remembrance of God. What do guilt and sickness, pain, disaster and all suffering mean now? Having no purpose, they are gone. And with them also go all the effects they seemed to cause. Cause and effect but replicate creation. Seen in their proper perspective, without distortion and without fear, they re-establish Heaven.

3. The function of the teacher of God

If the patient must change his mind in order to be healed, what does the teacher of God do? Can he change the patient's mind for him? Certainly not. For those already willing to change their minds he has no function except to rejoice with them, for they have become teachers of God with him. He has, however, a more specific function for those who do not understand what healing is. These patients do not realize they have chosen sickness. On the contrary, they believe that sickness has chosen them. Nor are they open-minded on this point. The body tells them what to do and they obey. They have no idea how insane this concept is. If they even suspected it, they would be healed. Yet they suspect nothing. To them the separation is quite real.

To them God's teachers come, to represent another choice which they had forgotten. The simple presence of a teacher of God is a reminder. His thoughts ask for the right to question what the patient has accepted as true. As God's messengers, His teachers are the symbols of salvation. They ask the patient for forgiveness for God's Son in his own Name. They stand for the Alternative. With God's Word in their minds they come in benediction, not to heal the sick but to remind them of the remedy God has already given them. It is not their hands that heal. It is not their voice that speaks the Word of God. They merely give what has been given them. Very gently they call to their brothers to turn away from death. Behold, you Son of God, what Life can offer you. Would you choose sickness in place of this?

Not once do the advanced teachers of God consider the forms of sickness in which their brother believes. To do this is to forget that all of them have the same purpose, and therefore are not really different. They seek for God's Voice in this brother who would so deceive himself as to believe God's Son can suffer. And they remind him that he did not make himself, and must remain as God created him. They recognize illusions can have no effect. The truth in their minds reaches out to the truth in the minds of their brothers, so that illusions are not reinforced. They are thus brought to truth; truth is not brought to them. So are they dispelled, not by the will of another, but by the One Will with Itself. And this is the function of God's teachers; to see no will as separate from their own, nor theirs as separate from God's.

IS HEALING CERTAIN?

Healing is always certain. It is impossible to let illusions be brought to truth and keep the illusions. Truth demonstrates illusions have no value. The teacher of God has seen the correction of his errors in the mind of the patient, recognizing it for what it is. Having accepted the Atonement for himself, he has also accepted it for the patient. Yet what if the patient uses sickness as a way of life, believing healing is the way to death? When this is so, a sudden healing might precipitate intense depression, and a sense of loss so deep that the patient might even try to destroy himself. Having nothing to live for, he may ask for death. Healing must wait, for his protection.

Healing will always stand aside when it would be seen as threat. The instant it is welcome it is there. Where healing has been given it will be received. And what is time before the gifts of God? We have referred many times in the text to the storehouse of treasures laid up equally for the giver and the receiver of God's gifts. Not one is lost, for they can but increase. No teacher of God should feel disappointed if he has offered healing and it does not appear to have been received. It is not up to him to judge when his gift should be accepted. Let him be certain it has been received, and trust that it will be accepted when it is recognized as a blessing and not a curse.

It is not the function of God's teachers to evaluate the outcome of their gifts. It is merely their function to give them. Once they have done that they have also given the outcome, for that is part of the gift. No one can give if he is concerned with the result of giving. That is a limitation on the giving itself, and neither the giver nor the receiver would have the gift. Trust is an essential part of giving; in fact, it is the part that makes sharing possible, the part that guarantees the giver will not lose, but only gain. Who gives a gift and then remains with it, to be sure it is used as the giver deems appropriate? Such is not giving but imprisoning.

It is the relinquishing of all concern about the gift that makes it truly given. And it is trust that makes true giving possible. Healing is the change of mind that the Holy Spirit in the patient's mind is seeking for him. And it is the Holy Spirit in the mind of the giver Who gives the gift to him. How can it be lost? How can it be ineffectual? How can it be wasted? God's treasure house can never be empty. And if one gift is missing, it would not be full. Yet is its fullness guaranteed by God. What concern, then, can a teacher of

God have about what becomes of his gifts? Given by God to God, who in this holy exchange can receive less than everything?

SHOULD HEALING BE REPEATED?

This question really answers itself. Healing cannot be repeated. If the patient is healed, what remains to heal him from? And if the healing is certain, as we have already said it is, what is there to repeat? For a teacher of God to remain concerned about the result of healing is to limit the healing. It is now the teacher of God himself whose mind needs to be healed. And it is this he must facilitate. He is now the patient, and he must so regard himself. He has made a mistake, and must be willing to change his mind about it. He lacked the trust that makes for giving truly, and so he has not received the benefit of his gift.

Whenever a teacher of God has tried to be a channel for healing he has succeeded. Should he be tempted to doubt this, he should not repeat his previous effort. That was already maximal, because the Holy Spirit so accepted it and so used it. Now the teacher of God has only one course to follow. He must use his reason to tell himself that he has given the problem to One Who cannot fail, and must recognize that his own uncertainty is not love but fear, and therefore hate. His position has thus become untenable, for he is offering hate to one to whom he offered love. This is impossible. Having offered love, only love can be received.

It is in this that the teacher of God must trust. This is what is really meant by the statement that the one responsibility of the miracle worker is to accept the Atonement for himself. The teacher of God is a miracle worker because he gives the gifts he has received. Yet he must first accept them. He need do no more, nor is there more that he could do. By accepting healing he can give it. If he doubts this, let him remember Who gave the gift and Who received it. Thus is his doubt corrected. He thought the gifts of God could be withdrawn. That was a mistake, but hardly one to stay with. And so the teacher of God can only recognize it for what it is, and let it be corrected for him.

One of the most difficult temptations to recognize is that to doubt a healing because of the appearance of continuing symptoms is a mistake in the form of lack of trust. As such it is an attack. Usually it seems to be just the opposite. It does appear unreasonable at first to be told that continued concern is attack. It has all the appearances of love. Yet love without trust is impossible, and doubt and trust cannot coexist. And hate must be the opposite of love, regardless of the form it takes. Doubt not the gift and it is impossible to doubt its result. This is the certainty that gives God's teachers the power to be miracle workers, for they have put their trust in Him.

The real basis for doubt about the outcome of any problem that has been given to God's Teacher for resolution is always self doubt. And that necessarily implies that trust has been placed in an illusory self, for only such a self can be doubted. This illusion can take many forms. Perhaps there is a fear of weakness and vulnerability. Perhaps there is a fear of failure and shame associated with a sense of inadequacy. Perhaps there is a guilty embarrassment stemming from false humility. The form of the mistake is not important. What is important is only the recognition of a mistake as a mistake.

The mistake is always some form of concern with the self to the exclusion of the patient. It is a failure to recognize him as part of the Self, and thus represents a confusion in identity. Conflict about what you are has entered your mind, and you have become deceived about yourself. And you are deceived about yourself because you have denied the Source of your creation. If you are offering only healing, you cannot doubt. Doubt is the result of conflicting wishes. Be sure of what you want, and doubt becomes impossible.

HOW CAN PERCEPTION OF ORDER OF DIFFICULTIES
BE AVOIDED?

The belief in order of difficulties is the basis for the world's perception. It rests on differences; on uneven background and shifting foreground, on unequal heights and diverse sizes, on varying degrees of darkness and light, and thousands of contrasts in which each thing seen competes with every other in order to be recognized. A larger object overshadows a smaller one. A brighter thing draws the attention from another with less intensity of appeal. And a more threatening idea, or one conceived of as more desirable by the world's standards, completely upsets the mental balance. What the body's eyes behold is only conflict. Look not to them for peace and understanding.

Illusions are always illusions of differences. How could it be otherwise? By definition, an illusion is an attempt to make something real that is regarded as of major importance, but is recognized as being untrue. The mind therefore seeks to make it true out of its intensity of desire to have it for itself. Illusions are travesties of creation; attempts to bring truth to lies. Finding truth unacceptable, the mind revolts against truth and gives itself an illusion of victory. Finding health a burden, it retreats into feverish dreams. And in these dreams the mind is separate, different from other minds, with different interests of its own, and able to gratify its needs at the expense of others.

It is in the sorting out and categorizing activities of the mind that errors in perception enter. And it is here correction must be made. The mind classifies what the body's eyes bring to it according to its preconceived values, judging where each sense datum fits best. What basis could be faultier than this? Unrecognized by itself, it has itself asked to be given what will fit into these categories. And having done so, it concludes that the categories must be true. On this the judgment of all differences rests, because it is on this that judgments of the world depend. Can this confused and senseless "reasoning" be depended on for anything?

There can be no order of difficulty in healing merely because all sickness is illusion. Is it harder to dispel the belief of the insane in a larger hallucination as opposed to a smaller one? Will he agree more quickly to the unreality of a louder voice he hears than to that of a softer one? Will he dismiss more easily a whispered demand to kill than a shout? And do the number of pitchforks the devils he sees carrying affect their credibility in his perception? His mind has categorized them all as real, and so they are all real to him. When he realizes they are all illusions they will disappear. And so it is with healing. The properties of illusions which seem to make them different are really irrelevant, for their properties are as illusory as they are.

The body's eyes will continue to see differences. But the mind that has let itself be healed will no longer acknowledge them. There will be those who seem to be "sicker" than others, and the body's eyes will report their changed appearances as before. But the healed mind will put them all in one category; they are unreal. This is the gift of its Teacher; the understanding that only two categories are meaningful in sorting out the messages the mind receives from what appears to be the outside world. And of these two, but one is real. Just as reality is wholly real, apart from size and shape and time and place — for differences cannot exist within it — so too are illusions without distinctions. The one answer to sickness of any kind is healing. The one answer to all illusions is truth.

ARE CHANGES REQUIRED IN THE LIFE SITUATION OF GOD'S TEACHERS?

Changes are required in the *minds* of God's teachers. This may or may not involve changes in the external situation. Remember that no one is where he is by accident, and chance plays no part in God's plan. It is most unlikely that changes in attitudes would not be the first step in the newly-made teacher of God's training. There is, however, no set pattern, since training is always highly individualized. There are those who are called upon to change their life situation almost immediately, but these are generally special cases. By far the majority are given a slowly-evolving training program, in which as many previous mistakes as possible are corrected. Relationships in particular must be properly perceived, and all dark cornerstones of unforgiveness removed. Otherwise the old thought system still has a basis for return.

As the teacher of God advances in his training, he learns one lesson with increasing thoroughness. He does not make his own decisions; he asks his Teacher for His answer, and it is this he follows as his guide for action. This becomes easier and easier, as the teacher of God learns to give up his own judgment. The giving up of judgment, the obvious prerequisite for hearing God's Voice, is usually a fairly slow process, not because it is difficult, but because it is apt to be perceived as personally insulting. The world's training is directed toward achieving a goal in direct opposition to that of our curriculum. The world trains for reliance on one's judgment as the criterion for maturity and strength. Our curriculum trains for the relinquishment of judgment as the necessary condition of salvation.

HOW IS JUDGMENT RELINQUISHED?

Judgment, like other devices by which the world of illusions is maintained, is totally misunderstood by the world. It is actually confused with wisdom, and substitutes for truth. As the world uses the term, an individual is capable of "good" and "bad" judgment, and his education aims at strengthening the former and minimizing the latter. There is, however, considerable confusion about what these categories mean. What is "good" judgment to one is "bad" judgment to another. Further, even the same person classifies the same action as showing "good" judgment at one time and "bad" judgment at another time. Nor can any consistent criteria for determining what these categories are be really taught. At any time the student may disagree with what his would-be teacher says about them, and the teacher himself may well be inconsistent in what he believes. "Good" judgment, in these terms, does not mean anything. No more does "bad."

It is necessary for the teacher of God to realize, not that he should not judge, but that he cannot. In giving up judgment, he is merely giving up what he did not have. He gives up an illusion; or better, he has an illusion of giving up. He has actually merely become more honest. Recognizing that judgment was always impossible for him, he no longer attempts it. This is no sacrifice. On the contrary, he puts himself in a position where judgment *through* him rather than *by* him can occur. And this judgment is neither "good" nor "bad." It is the only judgment there is, and it is only one: "God's Son is guiltless, and sin does not exist."

The aim of our curriculum, unlike the goal of the world's learning, is the recognition that judgment in the usual sense is impossible. This is not an opinion but a fact. In order to judge anything rightly, one would have to be fully aware of an inconceivably wide range of things; past, present and to come. One would have to recognize in advance all the effects of his judgments on everyone and everything involved in them in any way. And one would have to be certain there is no distortion in his perception, so that his judgment would be wholly fair to everyone on whom it rests now and in the future. Who is in a position to do this? Who except in grandiose fantasies would claim this for himself?

Remember how many times you thought you knew all the "facts" you needed for judgment, and how wrong you were! Is there anyone who has not had this experience? Would you know how many times you merely thought you were right, without ever realizing you were wrong? Why would you choose such an arbitrary basis for decision-making? Wisdom is not judgment; it is the relinquishment of judgment. Make then but one more judgment. It is this: There is Someone with you Whose judgment is perfect. He does know all the facts; past, present and to come. He does know all the effects of His judgment on everyone and everything involved in any way. And He is wholly fair to everyone, for there is no distortion in His perception.

Therefore lay judgment down, not with regret but with a sigh of gratitude. Now are you free of a burden so great that you could merely stagger and fall down beneath it. And it was all illusion. Nothing more. Now can the teacher of God rise up unburdened, and walk lightly on. Yet it is not only this that is his benefit. His sense of care is gone, for he has none. He has given it away, along with judgment. He gave himself to Him Whose judgment he has chosen now to trust, instead of his own. Now he makes no mistakes. His Guide is sure. And where he came to judge, he comes to bless. Where now he laughs, he used to come to weep.

It is not difficult to relinquish judgment. But it is difficult indeed to try to keep it. The teacher of God lays it down happily the instant he recognizes its cost. All of the ugliness he sees about him is its outcome. All of the pain he looks upon is its result. All of the loneliness and sense of loss; of passing time and growing hope-lessness; of sickening despair and fear of death; all these have come of it. And now he knows that these things need not be. Not one is true. For he has given up their cause, and they, which never were but the effects of his mistaken choice, have fallen from him. Teacher of God, this step will bring you peace. Can it be difficult to want but this?

HOW IS PEACE POSSIBLE IN THIS WORLD?

This is a question everyone must ask. Certainly peace seems to be impossible here. Yet the Word of God promises other things that seem impossible, as well as this. His Word has promised peace. It has also promised that there is no death, that resurrection must occur, and that rebirth is man's inheritance. The world you see cannot be the world God loves, and yet His Word assures us that He loves the world. God's Word has promised that peace is possible here, and what He promises can hardly be impossible. But it is true that the world must be looked at differently, if His promises are to be accepted. What the world is, is but a fact. You cannot choose what this should be. But you can choose how you would see it. Indeed, you *must* choose this.

Again we come to the question of judgment. This time ask yourself whether your judgment or the Word of God is more likely to be true. For they say different things about the world, and things so opposite that it is pointless to try to reconcile them. God offers the world salvation; your judgment would condemn it. God says there is no death; your judgment sees but death as the inevitable end of life. God's Word assures you that He loves the world; your judgment says it is unlovable. Who is right? For one of you is wrong. It must be so.

The text explains that the Holy Spirit is the Answer to all problems you have made. These problems are not real, but that is meaningless to those who believe in them. And everyone believes in what he made, for it was made by his believing it. Into this strange and paradoxical situation,—one without meaning and devoid of sense, yet out of which no way seems possible,—God has sent His Judgment to answer yours. Gently His Judgment substitutes for yours. And through this substitution is the un-understandable made understandable. How is peace possible in this world? In your judgment it is not possible, and can never be possible. But in the Judgment of God what is reflected here is only peace.

Peace is impossible to those who look on war. Peace is inevitable to those who offer peace. How easily, then, is your judgment of the world escaped! It is not the world that makes peace seem impossible. It is the world you see that is impossible. Yet has God's Judgment on this distorted world redeemed it and made it fit to welcome peace. And peace descends on it in joyous answer. Peace now belongs here, because a Thought of God has entered. What else but a Thought of God turns hell to Heaven merely by being what it is? The earth bows down before its gracious Presence, and it leans down in answer, to raise it up again. Now is the question different. It is no longer, "Can peace be possible in this world?" but instead, "Is it not impossible that peace be absent here?"

HOW MANY TEACHERS OF GOD ARE NEEDED TO
SAVE THE WORLD?

The answer to this question is — one. One wholly perfect teacher, whose learning is complete, suffices. This one, sanctified and redeemed, becomes the Self Who is the Son of God. He who was always wholly spirit now no longer sees himself as a body, or even as in a body. Therefore he is limitless. And being limitless, his thoughts are joined with God's forever and ever. His perception of himself is based upon God's Judgment, not his own. Thus does he share God's Will, and bring his thoughts to still deluded minds. He is forever one, because he is as God created him. He has accepted Christ, and he is saved.

Thus does the son of man become the Son of God. It is not really a change; it is a change of mind. Nothing external alters, but everything internal now reflects only the Love of God. God can no longer be feared, for the mind sees no cause for punishment. God's teachers appear to be many, for that is what is the world's need. Yet being joined in one purpose, and one they share with God, how could they be separate from each other? What does it matter if they then appear in many forms? Their minds are one; their joining is complete. And God works through them now as one, for that is what they are.

Why is the illusion of many necessary? Only because reality is not understandable to the deluded. Only very few can hear God's Voice at all, and even they cannot communicate His messages directly through the Spirit Which gave them. They need a medium through which communication becomes possible to those who do not realize that they are spirit. A body they can see. A voice they understand and listen to, without the fear that truth would en-counter in them. Do not forget that truth can come only where it is welcomed without fear. So do God's teachers need a body, for their unity could not be recognized directly.

Yet what makes God's teachers is their recognition of the proper purpose of the body. As they advance in their profession, they become more and more certain that the body's function is but to let God's Voice speak through it to human ears. And these ears will carry to the mind of the hearer messages that are not of this world, and the mind will understand because of their Source. From this understanding will come the recognition, in this new teacher of God, of what the body's purpose really is; the only use there really is for it. This lesson is enough to let the thought of unity come in, and what is one is recognized as one. The teachers of God appear to share the illusion of separation, but because of what they use the body for, they do not believe in the illusion despite appearances.

The central lesson is always this; that what you use the body for it will become to you. Use it for sin or for attack, which is the same as sin, and you will see it as sinful. Because it is sinful it is weak, and being weak, it suffers and it dies. Use it to bring the Word of God to those who have it not, and the body becomes holy. Because it is holy it cannot be sick, nor can it die. When its usefulness is done it is laid by, and that is all. The mind makes this decision, as it makes all decisions that are responsible for the body's condition. Yet the teacher of God does not make this decision alone. To do that would be to give the body another purpose from the one that keeps it holy. God's Voice will tell him when he has fulfilled his role, just as It tells him what his function is. He does not suffer either in going or remaining. Sickness is now impossible to him.

Oneness and sickness cannot coexist. God's teachers choose to look on dreams a while. It is a conscious choice. For they have learned that all choices are made consciously, with full awareness of their consequences. The dream says otherwise, but who would put his faith in dreams once they are recognized for what they are? Awareness of dreaming is the real function of God's teachers. They watch the dream figures come and go, shift and change, suffer and die. Yet they are not deceived by what they see. They recognize that to behold a dream figure as sick and separate is no more real than to regard it as healthy and beautiful. Unity alone is not a thing of dreams. And it is this God's teachers acknowledge as behind the dream, beyond all seeming and yet surely theirs.

WHAT IS THE REAL MEANING OF SACRIFICE?

Although in truth the term sacrifice is altogether meaningless, it does have meaning in the world. Like all things in the world, its meaning is temporary and will ultimately fade into the nothingness from which it came when there is no more use for it. Now its real meaning is a lesson. Like all lessons it is an illusion, for in reality there is nothing to learn. Yet this illusion must be replaced by a corrective device; another illusion that replaces the first, so both can finally disappear. The first illusion, which must be displaced before another thought system can take hold, is that it is a sacrifice to give up the things of this world. What could this be but an illusion, since this world itself is nothing more than that?

It takes great learning both to realize and to accept the fact that the world has nothing to give. What can the sacrifice of nothing mean? It cannot mean that you have less because of it. There is no sacrifice in the world's terms that does not involve the body. Think a while about what the world calls sacrifice. Power, fame, money, physical pleasure; who is the "hero" to whom all these things belong? Could they mean anything except to a body? Yet a body cannot evaluate. By seeking after such things the mind associates itself with the body, obscuring its identity and losing sight of what it really is.

Once this confusion has occurred, it becomes impossible for the mind to understand that all the "pleasures" of the world are nothing. But what a sacrifice,—and it is sacrifice indeed! —all this entails. Now has the mind condemned itself to seek without finding; to be forever dissatisfied and discontented; to know not what it really wants to find. Who can escape this self condemnation? Only through God's Word could this be possible. For self condemnation is a decision about identity, and no one doubts what he believes he is. He can doubt all things, but never this.

God's teachers can have no regret on giving up the pleasures of the world. Is it a sacrifice to give up pain? Does an adult resent the giving up of children's toys? Does one whose vision has already glimpsed the face of Christ look back with longing on a slaughter house? No one who has escaped the world and all its ills looks back on it with condemnation. Yet he must rejoice that he is free of all the sacrifice its values would demand of him. To them he sacrifices all his peace. To them he sacrifices all his freedom. And to possess them must he sacrifice his hope of Heaven and remembrance of his

Father's Love. Who in his sane mind chooses nothing as a substitute for everything?

What is the real meaning of sacrifice? It is the cost of believing in illusions. It is the price that must be paid for the denial of truth. There is no pleasure of the world that does not demand this, for otherwise the pleasure would be seen as pain, and no one asks for pain if he recognizes it. It is the idea of sacrifice that makes him blind. He does not see what he is asking for. And so he seeks it in a thousand ways and in a thousand places, each time believing it is there, and each time disappointed in the end. "Seek but do not find" remains this world's stern decree, and no one who pursues the world's goals can do otherwise.

You may believe this course requires sacrifice of all you really hold dear. In one sense this is true, for you hold dear the things that crucify God's Son, and it is the course's aim to set him free. But do not be mistaken about what sacrifice means. It always means the giving up of what you want. And what, O teacher of God, is it that you want? You have been called by God, and you have answered. Would you now sacrifice that Call? Few have heard it as yet, and they can but turn to you. There is no other hope in all the world that they can trust. There is no other voice in all the world that echoes God's. If you would sacrifice the truth, they stay in hell. And if they stay, you will remain with them.

Do not forget that sacrifice is total. There are no half sacrifices. You cannot give up Heaven partially. You cannot be a little bit in hell. The Word of God has no exceptions. It is this that makes it holy and beyond the world. It is its holiness that points to God. It is its holiness that makes you safe. It is denied if you attack any brother for anything. For it is here the split with God occurs. A split that is impossible. A split that cannot happen. Yet a split in which you surely will believe, because you have set up a situation that is impossible. And in this situation the impossible can seem to happen. It seems to happen at the "sacrifice" of truth.

Teacher of God, do not forget the meaning of sacrifice, and remember what each decision you make must mean in terms of cost. Decide for God, and everything is given you at no cost at all. Decide against Him, and you choose nothing, at the expense of the awareness of everything. What would you teach? Remember only what you would learn. For it is here that your concern should be. Atonement is for you. Your learning claims it and your learning gives it. The world contains it not. But learn this course and it is yours. God holds out His Word to you, for He has need of teachers. What other way is there to save His Son?

HOW WILL THE WORLD END?

Can what has no beginning really end? The world will end in an illusion, as it began. Yet will its ending be an illusion of mercy. The illusion of forgiveness, complete, excluding no one, limitless in gentleness, will cover it, hiding all evil, concealing all sin and ending guilt forever. So ends the world that guilt had made, for now it has no purpose and is gone. The father of illusions is the belief that they have a purpose; that they serve a need or gratify a want. Perceived as purposeless, they are no longer seen. Their uselessness is recognized, and they are gone. How but in this way are all illusions ended? They have been brought to truth, and truth saw them not. It merely overlooked the meaningless.

Until forgiveness is complete, the world does have a purpose. It becomes the home in which forgiveness is born, and where it grows and becomes stronger and more all-embracing. Here is it nourished, for here it is needed. A gentle Savior, born where sin was made and guilt seemed real. Here is His home, for here there is need of Him indeed. He brings the ending of the world with Him. It is His Call God's teachers answer, turning to Him in silence to receive His Word. The world will end when all things in it have been rightly judged by His judgment. The world will end with the benediction of holiness upon it. When not one thought of sin remains, the world is over. It will not be destroyed nor attacked nor even touched. It will merely cease to seem to be.

Certainly this seems to be a long, long while away. "When not one thought of sin remains" appears to be a long-range goal indeed. But time stands still, and waits on the goal of God's teachers. Not one thought of sin will remain the instant any one of them accepts Atonement for himself. It is not easier to forgive one sin than to forgive all of them. The illusion of orders of difficulty is an obstacle the teacher of God must learn to pass by and leave behind. One sin perfectly forgiven by one teacher of God can make salvation complete. Can you understand this? No; it is meaningless to anyone here. Yet it is the final lesson in which unity is restored. It goes against all the thinking of the world, but so does Heaven.

The world will end when its thought system has been completely reversed. Until then, bits and pieces of its thinking will still seem sensible. The final lesson, which brings the ending of the world, cannot be grasped by those not yet prepared to leave the world and go beyond its tiny reach. What, then, is the function of the teacher of God in this concluding lesson? He need merely learn how to approach it; to be willing to go in its direction. He need merely trust that, if God's Voice tells him it is a lesson he can learn, he can learn it. He does not judge it either as hard or easy. His Teacher points to it, and he trusts that He will show him how to learn it.

The world will end in joy, because it is a place of sorrow. When joy has come, the purpose of the world has gone. The world will end in peace, because it is a place of war. When peace has come, what is the purpose of the world? The world will end in laughter, because it is a place of tears. Where there is laughter, who can longer weep? And only complete forgiveness brings all this to bless the world. In blessing it departs, for it will not end as it began. To turn hell into Heaven is the function of God's teachers, for what they teach are lessons in which Heaven is reflected. And now sit down in true humility, and realize that all God would have you do you can do. Do not be arrogant and say you cannot learn His Own curriculum. His Word says otherwise. His Will be done. It cannot be otherwise. And be you thankful it is so.

IS EACH ONE TO BE JUDGED IN THE END?

Indeed, yes! No one can escape God's final judgment. Who could flee forever from the truth? But the final judgment will not come until it is no longer associated with fear. One day each one will welcome it, and on that very day it will be given him. He will hear his sinlessness proclaimed around and around the world, setting it free as God's final judgment on him is received. This is the judgment in which salvation lies. This is the judgment that will set him free. This is the judgment in which all things are freed with him. Time pauses as eternity comes near, and silence lies across the world that everyone may hear this judgment of the Son of God:

> *"Holy are you, eternal, free and whole,*
> *At peace forever in the Heart of God.*
> *Where is the world, and where is sorrow now?"*

Is this your judgment on yourself, teacher of God? Do you believe that this is wholly true? No; not yet, not yet. But this is still your goal; why you are here. It is your function to prepare yourself to hear this judgment and to recognize that it is true. One instant of complete belief in this, and you will go beyond belief to Certainty. One instant out of time can bring time's end. Judge not, for you but judge yourself, and thus delay this final judgment. What is your judgment of the world, teacher of God? Have you yet learned to stand aside and hear the Voice of Judgment in yourself? Or do you still attempt to take His role from Him? Learn to be quiet, for His Voice is heard in stillness. And His Judgment comes to all who stand aside in quiet listening, and wait for Him.

You who are sometimes sad and sometimes angry; who sometimes feel your just due is not given you, and your best efforts meet with lack of appreciation and even contempt; give up these foolish thoughts! They are too small and meaningless to occupy your holy mind an instant longer. God's Judgment waits for you to set you free. What can the world hold out to you, regardless of your judgments on its gifts, that you would rather have? You will be judged, and judged in fairness and in honesty. There is no deceit in God. His promises are sure. Only remember that. His promises have guaranteed His Judgment, and His alone, will be accepted in the end. It is your function to make that end be soon. It is your function to hold it to your heart, and offer it to all the world to keep it safe.

To the advanced teacher of God this question is meaningless. There is no program, for the lessons change each day. Yet the teacher of God is sure of but one thing; they do not change at random. Seeing this and understanding that it is true, he rests content. He will be told all that his role should be, this day and every day. And those who share that role with him will find him, so they can learn the lessons for the day together. Not one is absent whom he needs; not one is sent without a learning goal already set, and one which can be learned that very day. For the advanced teacher of God, then, this question is superfluous. It has been asked and answered, and he keeps in constant contact with the Answer. He is set, and sees the road on which he walks stretch surely and smoothly before him.

But what about those who have not reached his certainty? They are not yet ready for such lack of structuring on their own part. What must they do to learn to give the day to God? There are some general rules which do apply, although each one must use them as best he can in his own way. Routines as such are dangerous, because they easily become gods in their own right, threatening the very goals for which they were set up. Broadly speaking, then, it can be said that it is well to start the day right. It is always possible to begin again, should the day begin with error. Yet there are obvious advantages in terms of saving time.

At the beginning, it is wise to think in terms of time. This is by no means the ultimate criterion, but at the outset it is probably the simplest to observe. The saving of time is an essential early emphasis which, although it remains important throughout the learning process, becomes less and less emphasized. At the outset, we can safely say that time devoted to starting the day right does indeed save time. How much time should be so spent? This must depend on the teacher of God himself. He cannot claim that title until he has gone through the workbook, since we are learning within the framework of our course. After completion of the more structured practice periods, which the workbook contains, individual need becomes the chief consideration.

This course is always practical. It may be that the teacher of God is not in a situation that fosters quiet thought as he awakes. If this is so, let him but remember that he chooses to spend time with God as soon as possible, and let him do so. Duration is not the major concern. One can easily sit still an hour with closed eyes and accomplish nothing. One can as easily give God only an instant, and in that instant join with Him completely. Perhaps the one generalization that can be made is this; as soon as possible after waking take your quiet time, continuing a minute or two after you begin to find it difficult. You may find that the difficulty will diminish and drop away. If not, that is the time to stop.

The same procedures should be followed at night. Perhaps your quiet time should be fairly early in the evening, if it is not feasible for you to take it just before going to sleep. It is not wise to lie down for it. It is better to sit up, in whatever position you prefer. Having gone through the workbook, you must have come to some conclusions in this respect. If possible, however, just before going to sleep is a desirable time to devote to God. It sets your mind into a pattern of rest, and orients you away from fear. If it is expedient to spend this time earlier, at least be sure that you do not forget a brief period,—not more than a moment will do,—in which you close your eyes and think of God.

There is one thought in particular that should be remembered throughout the day. It is a thought of pure joy; a thought of peace, a thought of limitless release, limitless because all things are freed within it. You think you made a place of safety for yourself. You think you made a power that can save you from all the fearful things you see in dreams. It is not so. Your safety lies not there. What you give up is merely the illusion of protecting illusions. And it is this you fear, and only this. How foolish to be so afraid of nothing! Nothing at all! Your defenses will not work, but you are not in danger. You have no need of them. Recognize this, and they will disappear. And only then will you accept your real protection.

How simply and how easily does time slip by for the teacher of God who has accepted His protection! All that he did before in the name of safety no longer interests him. For he is safe, and knows it to be so. He has a Guide Who will not fail. He need make no distinctions among the problems he perceives, for He to Whom he turns with all of them recognizes no order of difficulty in resolving them. He is as safe in the present as he was before illusions were accepted into his mind, and as he will be when he has let them go. There is no difference in his state at different times and different places, because they are all one to God. This is his safety. And he has no need for more than this.

Yet there will be temptations along the way the teacher of God has yet to travel, and he has need of reminding himself throughout the day of his protection. How can he do this, particularly during the time when his mind is occupied with external things? He can but try, and his success depends on his conviction that he will succeed. He must be sure success is not of him, but will be given him at any time, in any place and circumstance he calls for it. There are times his certainty will waver, and the instant this occurs he will return to earlier attempts to place reliance on himself alone. Forget not this is magic, and magic is a sorry substitute for true assistance. It is not good enough for God's teacher, because it is not enough for God's Son.

The avoidance of magic is the avoidance of temptation. For all temptation is nothing more than the attempt to substitute another will for God's. These attempts may indeed seem frightening, but they are merely pathetic. They can have no effects; neither good nor bad, neither rewarding nor demanding sacrifice, healing nor destructive, quieting nor fearful. When all magic is recognized as merely nothing, the teacher of God has reached the most advanced state. All intermediate lessons will but lead to this, and bring this goal nearer to recognition. For magic of any kind, in all its forms, simply does nothing. Its powerlessness is the reason it can be so easily escaped. What has no effects can hardly terrify.

There is no substitute for the Will of God. In simple statement, it is to this fact that the teacher of God devotes his day. Each substitute he may accept as real can but deceive him. But he is safe from all deception if he so decides. Perhaps he needs to remember, "God is with me. I cannot be deceived." Perhaps he prefers other words, or only one, or none at all. Yet each temptation to accept magic as true must be abandoned through his recognition, not that it is fearful, not that it is sinful, not that it is dangerous, but merely that it is meaningless. Rooted in sacrifice and separation, two aspects of one error and no more, he merely chooses to give up all that he never had. And for this "sacrifice" is Heaven restored to his awareness.

Is not this an exchange that you would want? The world would gladly make it, if it knew it could be made. It is God's teachers who must teach it that it can. And so it is their function to make sure that they have learned it. No risk is possible throughout the day except to put your trust in magic, for it is only this that leads to pain. "There is no will but God's." His teachers know that this is so, and have learned that everything but this is magic. All belief in magic is maintained by just one simple-minded illusion;—that it works. All through his training, every day and every hour, and even every minute and second, must God's teachers learn to recognize the forms of magic and perceive their meaninglessness. Fear is withdrawn from them, and so they go. And thus the gate of Heaven is reopened, and its light can shine again on an untroubled mind.

HOW DO GOD'S TEACHERS DEAL WITH
MAGIC THOUGHTS?

This is a crucial question both for teacher and pupil. If this issue is mishandled, the teacher of God has hurt himself and has also attacked his pupil. This strengthens fear, and makes the magic seem quite real to both of them. How to deal with magic thus becomes a major lesson for the teacher of God to master. His first responsibility in this is not to attack it. If a magic thought arouses anger in any form, God's teacher can be sure that he is strengthening his own belief in sin and has condemned himself. He can be sure as well that he has asked for depression, pain, fear and disaster to come to him. Let him remember, then, it is not this that he would teach, because it is not this that he would learn.

There is, however, a temptation to respond to magic in a way that reinforces it. Nor is this always obvious. It can, in fact, be easily concealed beneath a wish to help. It is this double wish that makes the help of little value, and must lead to undesired outcomes. Nor should it be forgotten that the outcome that results will always come to teacher and to pupil alike. How many times has it been emphasized that you give but to yourself? And where could this be better shown than in the kinds of help the teacher of God gives to those who need his aid? Here is his gift most clearly given him. For he will give only what he has chosen for himself. And in this gift is his judgment upon the holy Son of God.

It is easiest to let error be corrected where it is most apparent, and errors can be recognized by their results. A lesson truly taught can lead to nothing but release for teacher and pupil, who have shared in one intent. Attack can enter only if perception of separate goals has entered. And this must indeed have been the case if the result is anything but joy. The single aim of the teacher turns the divided goal of the pupil into one direction, with the call for help becoming his one appeal. This then is easily responded to with just one answer, and this answer will enter the teacher's mind unfailingly. From there it shines into his pupil's mind, making it one with his.

Perhaps it will be helpful to remember that no one can be angry at a fact. It is always an interpretation that gives rise to negative emotions, regardless of their seeming justification by what *appears* as facts. Regardless, too, of the intensity of the anger that is aroused. It may be merely slight irritation, perhaps too mild to be even clearly recognized. Or it may also take the form of intense rage, accompanied by thoughts of violence, fantasied or apparently acted out. It does not matter. All of these reactions are the same. They obscure the truth, and this can never be a matter of degree. Either truth is apparent, or it is not. It cannot be partially recognized. Who is unaware of truth must look upon illusions.

Anger in response to perceived magic thoughts is a basic cause of fear. Consider what this reaction means, and its centrality in the world's thought system becomes apparent. A magic thought, by its mere presence, acknowledges a separation from God. It states, in the clearest form possible, that the mind which believes it has a separate will that can oppose the Will of God, also believes it can succeed. That this can hardly be a fact is obvious. Yet that it can be believed as fact is equally obvious. And herein lies the birthplace of guilt. Who usurps the place of God and takes it for himself now has a deadly "enemy." And he must stand alone in his protection, and make himself a shield to keep him safe from fury that can never be abated, and vengeance that can never be satisfied.

How can this unfair battle be resolved? Its ending is inevitable, for its outcome must be death. How, then, can one believe in one's defenses? Magic again must help. Forget the battle. Accept it as a fact, and then forget it. Do not remember the impossible odds against you. Do not remember the immensity of the "enemy," and do not think about your frailty in comparison. Accept your separation, but do not remember how it came about. Believe that you have won it, but do not retain the slightest memory of Who your great "opponent" really is. Projecting your "forgetting" onto Him, it seems to you He has forgotten, too.

But what will now be your reaction to all magic thoughts? They can but reawaken sleeping guilt, which you have hidden but have not let go. Each one says clearly to your frightened mind, "You have usurped the place of God. Think not He has forgotten." Here we have the fear of God most starkly represented. For in that thought has guilt already raised madness to the throne of God Himself. And now there is no hope. Except to kill. Here is salvation now. An angry father pursues his guilty son. Kill or be killed, for here alone is choice. Beyond this there is none, for what was done cannot be done without. The stain of blood can never be removed, and anyone who bears this stain on him must meet with death.

Into this hopeless situation God sends His teachers. They bring the light of hope from God Himself. There is a way in which escape is possible. It can be learned and taught, but it requires patience and abundant willingness. Given that, the lesson's manifest simplicity stands out like an intense white light against a black horizon, for such it is. If anger comes from an interpretation and not a fact, it is never justified. Once this is even dimly grasped, the way is open. Now it is possible to take the next step. The interpretation can be changed at last. Magic thoughts need not lead to condemnation, for they do not really have the power to give rise to guilt. And so they can be overlooked, and thus forgotten in the truest sense.

Madness but seems terrible. In truth it has no power to make anything. Like the magic which becomes its servant, it neither attacks nor protects. To see it and to recognize its thought system is to look on nothing. Can nothing give rise to anger? Hardly so. Remember, then, teacher of God, that anger recognizes a reality that is not there; yet is the anger certain witness that you do believe in it as fact. Now is escape impossible, until you see you have responded to your own interpretation, which you have projected on an outside world. Let this grim sword be taken from you now. There is no death. This sword does not exist. The fear of God is causeless. But His Love is Cause of everything beyond all fear, and thus forever real and always true.

Correction of a lasting nature,—and only this is true correction, —cannot be made until the teacher of God has ceased to confuse interpretation with fact, or illusion with truth. If he argues with his pupil about a magic thought, attacks it, tries to establish its error or demonstrate its falsity, he is but witnessing to its reality. Depression is then inevitable, for he has "proved," both to his pupil and himself, that it is their task to escape from what is real. And this can only be impossible. Reality is changeless. Magic thoughts are but illusions. Otherwise salvation would be only the same age-old impossible dream in but another form. Yet the dream of salvation has new content. It is not the form alone in which the difference lies.

God's teachers' major lesson is to learn how to react to magic thoughts wholly without anger. Only in this way can they proclaim the truth about themselves. Through them, the Holy Spirit can now speak of the reality of the Son of God. Now He can remind the world of sinlessness, the one unchanged, unchangeable condition of all that God created. Now He can speak the Word of God to listening ears, and bring Christ's vision to eyes that see. Now is He free to teach all minds the truth of what they are, so they will gladly be returned to Him. And now is guilt forgiven, overlooked completely in His sight and in God's Word.

Anger but screeches, "Guilt is real!" Reality is blotted out as this insane belief is taken as replacement for God's Word. The body's eyes now "see"; its ears alone can "hear." Its little space and tiny breath become the measure of reality. And truth becomes diminutive and meaningless. Correction has one answer to all this, and to the world that rests on this:

> "You but mistake interpretation for the truth. And you
> are wrong. But a mistake is not a sin, nor has reality
> been taken from its throne by your mistakes. God
> reigns forever, and His laws alone prevail upon you
> and upon the world. His Love remains the only thing
> there is. Fear is illusion, for you are like Him."

In order to heal, it thus becomes essential for the teacher of God to let all his own mistakes be corrected. If he senses even the faintest hint of irritation in himself as he responds to anyone, let him instantly realize that he has made an interpretation that is not true.

Then let him turn within to his Eternal Guide, and let Him judge what the response should be. So is he healed, and in his healing is his pupil healed with him. The sole responsibility of God's teacher is to accept the Atonement for himself. Atonement means correction, or the undoing of errors. When this has been accomplished, the teacher of God becomes a miracle worker by definition. His sins have been forgiven him, and he no longer condemns himself. How can he then condemn anyone? And who is there whom his forgiveness can fail to heal?

WHAT IS JUSTICE?

Justice is the divine correction for injustice. Injustice is the basis for all the judgments of the world. Justice corrects the interpretations to which injustice gives rise, and cancels them out. Neither justice nor injustice exists in Heaven, for error is impossible and correction meaningless. In this world, however, forgiveness depends on justice, since all attack can only be unjust. Justice is the Holy Spirit's verdict upon the world. Except in His judgment justice is impossible, for no one in the world is capable of making only just interpretations and laying all injustices aside. If God's Son were fairly judged, there would be no need for salvation. The thought of separation would have been forever inconceivable.

Justice, like its opposite, is an interpretation. It is, however, the one interpretation that leads to truth. This becomes possible because, while it is not true in itself, justice includes nothing that opposes truth. There is no inherent conflict between justice and truth; one is but the first small step in the direction of the other. The path becomes quite different as one goes along. Nor could all the magnificence, the grandeur of the scene and the enormous opening vistas that rise to meet one as the journey continues, be foretold from the outset. Yet even these, whose splendor reaches indescribable heights as one proceeds, fall short indeed of all that wait when the pathway ceases and time ends with it. But somewhere one must start. Justice is the beginning.

All concepts of your brothers and yourself; all fears of future states and all concerns about the past, stem from injustice. Here is the lens which, held before the body's eyes, distorts perception and brings witness of the distorted world back to the mind that made the lens and holds it very dear. Selectively and arbitrarily is every concept of the world built up in just this way. "Sins" are perceived and justified by careful selectivity in which all thought of wholeness must be lost. Forgiveness has no place in such a scheme, for not one "sin" but seems forever true.

Salvation is God's justice. It restores to your awareness the wholeness of the fragments you perceive as broken off and separate. And it is this that overcomes the fear of death. For separate fragments must decay and die, but wholeness is immortal. It remains forever and forever like its Creator, being one with Him. God's Judgment is His justice. Onto this,—a Judgment wholly lacking in condemnation; an evaluation based entirely on love,

—you have projected your injustice, giving God the lens of warped perception through which you look. Now it belongs to Him and not to you. You are afraid of Him, and do not see you hate and fear your Self as enemy.

Pray for God's justice, and do not confuse His mercy with your own insanity. Perception can make whatever picture the mind desires to see. Remember this. In this lies either Heaven or hell, as you elect. God's justice points to Heaven just because it is entirely impartial. It accepts all evidence that is brought before it, omitting nothing and assessing nothing as separate and apart from all the rest. From this one standpoint does it judge, and this alone. Here all attack and condemnation becomes meaningless and indefensible. Perception rests, the mind is still, and light returns again. Vision is now restored. What had been lost has now been found. The peace of God descends on all the world, and we can see. And we can see!

WHAT IS THE PEACE OF GOD?

It has been said that there is a kind of peace that is not of this world. How is it recognized? How is it found? And being found, how can it be retained? Let us consider each of these questions separately, for each reflects a different step along the way.

First, how can the peace of God be recognized? God's peace is recognized at first by just one thing; in every way it is totally unlike all previous experiences. It calls to mind nothing that went before. It brings with it no past associations. It is a new thing entirely. There is a contrast, yes, between this thing and all the past. But strangely, it is not a contrast of true differences. The past just slips away, and in its place is everlasting quiet. Only that. The contrast first perceived has merely gone. Quiet has reached to cover everything.

How is this quiet found? No one can fail to find it who but seeks out its conditions. God's peace can never come where anger is, for anger must deny that peace exists. Who sees anger as justified in any way or any circumstance proclaims that peace is meaningless, and must believe that it cannot exist. In this condition, peace cannot be found. Therefore, forgiveness is the necessary condition for finding the peace of God. More than this, given forgiveness there *must* be peace. For what except attack will lead to war? And what but peace is opposite to war? Here the initial contrast stands out clear and apparent. Yet when peace is found, the war is meaningless. And it is conflict now that is perceived as nonexistent and unreal.

How is the peace of God retained, once it is found? Returning anger, in whatever form, will drop the heavy curtain once again, and the belief that peace cannot exist will certainly return. War is again accepted as the one reality. Now must you once again lay down your sword, although you do not recognize that you have picked it up again. But you will learn, as you remember even faintly now that happiness was yours without it, that you must have taken it again as your defense. Stop for a moment now and think of this: Is conflict what you want, or is God's peace the better choice? Which gives you more? A tranquil mind is not a little gift. Would you not rather live than choose to die?

Living is joy, but death can only weep. You see in death escape from what you made. But this you do not see; that you made death, and it is but illusion of an end. Death cannot be escape, because it is not life in which the problem lies. Life has no opposite, for it is God. Life and death seem to be opposites because you have decided death ends life. Forgive the world, and you will understand that every thing that God created cannot have an end, and nothing He did not create is real. In this one sentence is our course explained. In this one sentence is our practicing given its one direction. And in this one sentence is the Holy Spirit's whole curriculum specified exactly as it is.

What is the peace of God? No more than this; the simple understanding that His Will is wholly without opposite. There is no thought that contradicts His Will, yet can be true. The contrast between His Will and yours but seemed to be reality. In truth there was no conflict, for His Will is yours. Now is the mighty Will of God Himself His gift to you. He does not seek to keep it for Himself. Why would you seek to keep your tiny frail imaginings apart from Him? The Will of God is one and all there is. This is your heritage. The universe beyond the sun and stars, and all the thoughts of which you can conceive, belong to you. God's peace is the condition for His Will. Attain His peace, and you remember Him.

WHAT IS THE ROLE OF WORDS IN HEALING?

Strictly speaking, words play no part at all in healing. The motivating factor is prayer, or asking. What you ask for you receive. But this refers to the prayer of the heart, not to the words you use in praying. Sometimes the words and the prayer are contradictory; sometimes they agree. It does not matter. God does not understand words, for they were made by separated minds to keep them in the illusion of separation. Words can be helpful, particularly for the beginner, in helping concentration and facilitating the exclusion, or at least the control, of extraneous thoughts Let us not forget, however, that words are but symbols of symbols They are thus twice removed from reality.

As symbols, words have quite specific references. Even when they seem most abstract, the picture that comes to mind is apt to be very concrete. Unless a specific referent does occur to the mind in conjunction with the word, the word has little or no practical meaning, and thus cannot help the healing process. The prayer of the heart does not really ask for concrete things. It always requests some kind of experience, the specific things asked for being the bringers of the desired experience in the opinion of the asker. The words, then, are symbols for the things asked for, but the things themselves but stand for the experiences that are hoped for.

The prayer for things of this world will bring experiences of this world. If the prayer of the heart asks for this, this will be given because this will be received. It is impossible that the prayer of the heart remain unanswered in the perception of the one who asks. If he asks for the impossible, if he wants what does not exist or seeks for illusions in his heart, all this becomes his own. The power of his decision offers it to him as he requests. Herein lie hell and Heaven. The sleeping Son of God has but this power left to him. It is enough. His words do not matter. Only the Word of God has any meaning, because it symbolizes that which has no human symbols at all. The Holy Spirit alone understands what this Word stands for. And this, too, is enough.

Is the teacher of God, then, to avoid the use of words in his teaching? No, indeed! There are many who must be reached through words, being as yet unable to hear in silence. The teacher of God must, however, learn to use words in a new way. Gradually, he learns how to let his words be chosen for him by ceasing to decide for himself what he will say. This process is merely a special case of the lesson in the workbook that says, "I will step back and let Him lead the way." The teacher of God accepts the words which are offered him, and gives as he receives. He does not control the direction of his speaking. He listens and hears and speaks.

A major hindrance in this aspect of his learning is the teacher of God's fear about the validity of what he hears. And what he hears may indeed be quite startling. It may also seem to be quite irrelevant to the presented problem as he perceives it, and may, in fact, confront the teacher with a situation that appears to be very embarrassing to him. All these are judgments that have no value. They are his own, coming from a shabby self-perception which he would leave behind. Judge not the words that come to you, but offer them in confidence. They are far wiser than your own. God's teachers have God's Word behind their symbols. And He Himself gives to the words they use the power of His Spirit, raising them from meaningless symbols to the Call of Heaven itself.

HOW ARE HEALING AND ATONEMENT RELATED?

Healing and Atonement are not related; they are identical. There is no order of difficulty in miracles because there are no degrees of Atonement. It is the one complete concept possible in this world, because it is the source of a wholly unified perception. Partial Atonement is a meaningless idea, just as special areas of hell in Heaven are inconceivable. Accept Atonement and you are healed. Atonement is the Word of God. Accept His Word and what remains to make sickness possible? Accept His Word and every miracle has been accomplished. To forgive is to heal. The teacher of God has taken accepting the Atonement for himself as his only function. What is there, then, he cannot heal? What miracle can be withheld from him?

The progress of the teacher of God may be slow or rapid, depending on whether he recognizes the Atonement's inclusiveness, or for a time excludes some problem areas from it. In some cases, there is a sudden and complete awareness of the perfect applicability of the lesson of the Atonement to all situations, but this is comparatively rare. The teacher of God may have accepted the function God has given him long before he has learned all that his acceptance holds out to him. It is only the end that is certain. Anywhere along the way, the necessary realization of inclusiveness may reach him. If the way seems long, let him be content. He has decided on the direction he wants to take. What more was asked of him? And having done what was required, would God withhold the rest?

That forgiveness is healing needs to be understood, if the teacher of God is to make progress. The idea that a body can be sick is a central concept in the ego's thought system. This thought gives the body autonomy, separates it from the mind, and keeps the idea of attack inviolate. If the body could be sick Atonement would be impossible. A body that can order a mind to do as it sees fit could merely take the place of God and prove salvation is impossible. What, then, is left to heal? The body has become lord of the mind. How could the mind be returned to the Holy Spirit unless the body is killed? And who would want salvation at such a price?

Certainly sickness does not appear to be a decision. Nor would anyone actually believe he wants to be sick. Perhaps he can accept the idea in theory, but it is rarely if ever consistently applied to all specific forms of sickness, both in the individual's perception of

53

himself and of all others as well. Nor is it at this level that the teacher of God calls forth the miracle of healing. He overlooks the mind *and* body, seeing only the face of Christ shining in front of him, correcting all mistakes and healing all perception. Healing is the result of the recognition, by God's teacher, of who it is that is in need of healing. This recognition has no special reference. It is true of all things that God created. In it are all illusions healed.

When a teacher of God fails to heal, it is because he has forgotten Who he is. Another's sickness thus becomes his own. In allowing this to happen, he has identified with another's ego, and has thus confused him with a body. In so doing, he has refused to accept the Atonement for himself, and can hardly offer it to his brother in Christ's Name. He will, in fact, be unable to recognize his brother at all, for his Father did not create bodies, and so he is seeing in his brother only the unreal. Mistakes do not correct mistakes, and distorted perception does not heal. Step back now, teacher of God. You have been wrong. Lead not the way, for you have lost it. Turn quickly to your Teacher, and let yourself be healed.

The offer of Atonement is universal. It is equally applicable to all individuals in all circumstances. And in it is the power to heal all individuals of all forms of sickness. Not to believe this is to be unfair to God, and thus unfaithful to Him. A sick person perceives himself as separate from God. Would you see him as separate from you? It is your task to heal the sense of separation that has made him sick. It is your function to recognize for him that what he believes about himself is not the truth. It is your forgiveness that must show him this. Healing is very simple. Atonement is received and offered. Having been received, it must be accepted. It is in the receiving, then, that healing lies. All else must follow from this single purpose.

Who can limit the power of God Himself? Who, then, can say which one can be healed of what, and what must remain beyond God's power to forgive? This is insanity indeed. It is not up to God's teachers to set limits upon Him, because it is not up to them to judge His Son. And to judge His Son is to limit his Father. Both are equally meaningless. Yet this will not be understood until God's teacher recognizes that they are the same mistake. Herein does he receive Atonement, for he withdraws his judgment from the Son of God, accepting him as God created him. No longer does he stand apart from God, determining where healing should be given and where it should be withheld. Now can he say with God, "This is my beloved Son, created perfect and forever so."

54

God's gifts can rarely be received directly. Even the most advanced of God's teachers will give way to temptation in this world. Would it be fair if their pupils were denied healing because of this? The Bible says, "Ask in the Name of Jesus Christ." Is this merely an appeal to magic? A name does not heal, nor does an invocation call forth any special power. What does it mean to call on Jesus Christ? What does calling on his Name confer? Why is the appeal to him part of healing?

We have repeatedly said that one who has perfectly accepted the Atonement for himself can heal the world. Indeed, he has already done so. Temptation may recur to others, but never to this One. He has become the risen Son of God. He has overcome death because he has accepted Life. He has recognized himself as God created him, and in so doing he has recognized all living things as part of him. There is now no limit on his power, because it is the Power of God. So has his name become the Name of God, for he no longer sees himself as separate from Him.

What does this mean for you? It means that in remembering Jesus you are remembering God. The whole relationship of the Son to the Father lies in him. His part in the Sonship is also yours, and his completed learning guarantees your own success. Is he still available for help? What did he say about this? Remember his promises, and ask yourself honestly whether it is likely that he will fail to keep them. Can God fail His Son? And can one who is one with God be unlike Him? Who transcends the body has transcended limitation. Would the greatest teacher be unavailable to those who follow him?

The Name of Jesus Christ as such is but a symbol. But it stands for love that is not of this world. It is a symbol that is safely used as a replacement for the many names of all the gods to which you pray. It becomes the shining symbol for the Word of God, so close to what it stands for that the little space between the two is lost, the moment that the Name is called to mind. Remembering the Name of Jesus Christ is to give thanks for all the gifts that God has given you. And gratitude to God becomes the way in which He is remembered, for love cannot be far behind a grateful heart and thankful mind. God enters easily, for these are the true conditions for your homecoming.

Jesus has led the way. Why would you not be grateful to him? He has asked for love, but only that he might give it to you. You do not love yourself. But in his eyes your loveliness is so complete and flawless that he sees in it an image of his Father. You become the symbol of his Father here on earth. To you he looks for hope, because in you he sees no limit and no stain to mar your beautiful perfection. In his eyes Christ's vision shines in perfect constancy. He has remained with you. Would you not learn the lesson of salvation through his learning? Why would you choose to start again, when he has made the journey for you?

No one on earth can grasp what Heaven is, or what its one Creator really means. Yet we have witnesses. It is to them that wisdom should appeal. There have been those whose learning far exceeds what we can learn. Nor would we teach the limitations we have laid on us. No one who has become a true and dedicated teacher of God forgets his brothers. Yet what he can offer them is limited by what he learns himself. Then turn to one who laid all limits by, and went beyond the farthest reach of learning. He will take you with him, for he did not go alone. And you were with him then, as you are now.

This course has come from him because his words have reached you in a language you can love and understand. Are other teachers possible, to lead the way to those who speak in different tongues and appeal to different symbols? Certainly there are. Would God leave anyone without a very present help in time of trouble; a savior who can symbolize Himself? Yet do we need a many-faceted curriculum, not because of content differences, but because symbols must shift and change to suit the need. Jesus has come to answer yours. In him you find God's Answer. Do you, then, teach with him, for he is with you; he is always here.

IS REINCARNATION SO?

In the ultimate sense, reincarnation is impossible. There is no past or future, and the idea of birth into a body has no meaning either once or many times. Reincarnation cannot, then, be true in any real sense. Our only question should be, "Is the concept helpful?" And that depends, of course, on what it is used for. If it is used to strengthen the recognition of the eternal nature of life, it is helpful indeed. Is any other question about it really useful in lighting up the way? Like many other beliefs, it can be bitterly misused. At least, such misuse offers preoccupation and perhaps pride in the past. At worst, it induces inertia in the present. In between, many kinds of folly are possible.

Reincarnation would not, under any circumstances, be the problem to be dealt with *now*. If it were responsible for some of the difficulties the individual faces now, his task would still be only to escape from them now. If he is laying the groundwork for a future life, he can still work out his salvation only now. To some, there may be comfort in the concept, and if it heartens them its value is self-evident. It is certain, however, that the way to salvation can be found by those who believe in reincarnation and by those who do not. The idea cannot, therefore, be regarded as essential to the curriculum. There is always some risk in seeing the present in terms of the past. There is always some good in any thought which strengthens the idea that life and the body are not the same.

For our purposes, it would not be helpful to take any definite stand on reincarnation. A teacher of God should be as helpful to those who believe in it as to those who do not. If a definite stand were required of him, it would merely limit his usefulness, as well as his own decision-making. Our course is not concerned with any concept that is not acceptable to anyone, regardless of his formal beliefs. His ego will be enough for him to cope with, and it is not the part of wisdom to add sectarian controversies to his burdens. Nor would there be an advantage in his premature acceptance of the course merely because it advocates a long-held belief of his own.

It cannot be too strongly emphasized that this course aims at a complete reversal of thought. When this is finally accomplished, issues such as the validity of reincarnation become meaningless. Until then, they are likely to be merely controversial. The teacher of God is, therefore, wise to step away from all such questions, for he has much to teach and learn apart from them. He should both learn and teach that theoretical issues but waste time, draining it away from its appointed purpose. If there are aspects to any concept or belief that will be helpful, he will be told about it. He will also be told how to use it. What more need he know?

Does this mean that the teacher of God should not believe in reincarnation himself, or discuss it with others who do? The answer is, certainly not! If he does believe in reincarnation, it would be a mistake for him to renounce the belief unless his internal Teacher so advised. And this is most unlikely. He might be advised that he is misusing the belief in some way that is detrimental to his pupil's advance or his own. Reinterpretation would then be recommended, because it is necessary. All that must be recognized, however, is that birth was not the beginning, and death is not the end. Yet even this much is not required of the beginner. He need merely accept the idea that what he knows is not necessarily all there is to learn. His journey has begun.

The emphasis of this course always remains the same; —it is at this moment that complete salvation is offered you, and it is at this moment that you can accept it. This is still your one responsibility. Atonement might be equated with total escape from the past and total lack of interest in the future. Heaven is here. There is nowhere else. Heaven is now. There is no other time. No teaching that does not lead to this is of concern to God's teachers. All beliefs will point to this if properly interpreted. In this sense, it can be said that their truth lies in their usefulness. All beliefs that lead to progress should be honored. This is the sole criterion this course requires. No more than this is necessary.

ARE "PSYCHIC" POWERS DESIRABLE?

The answer to this question is much like the preceding one. There are, of course, no "unnatural" powers, and it is obviously merely an appeal to magic to make up a power that does not exist. It is equally obvious, however, that each individual has many abilities of which he is unaware. As his awareness increases, he may well develop abilities that seem quite startling to him. Yet nothing he can do can compare even in the slightest with the glorious surprise of re-membering Who he is. Let all his learning and all his efforts be directed toward this one great final surprise, and he will not be content to be delayed by the little ones that may come to him on the way.

Certainly there are many "psychic" powers that are clearly in line with this course. Communication is not limited to the small range of channels the world recognizes. If it were, there would be little point in trying to teach salvation. It would be impossible to do so. The limits the world places on communication are the chief barriers to direct experience of the Holy Spirit, Whose Presence is always there and Whose Voice is available but for the hearing. These limits are placed out of fear, for without them the walls that surround all the separate places of the world would fall at the holy sound of His Voice. Who transcends these limits in any way is merely becoming more natural. He is doing nothing special, and there is no magic in his accomplishments.

The seemingly new abilities that may be gathered on the way can be very helpful. Given to the Holy Spirit, and used under His direction, they are valuable teaching aids. To this, the question of how they arise is irrelevant. The only important consideration is how they are used. Taking them as ends in themselves, no matter how this is done, will delay progress. Nor does their value lie in proving anything; achievements from the past, unusual attunement with the "unseen," or "special" favors from God. God gives no special favors, and no one has any powers that are not available to everyone. Only by tricks of magic are special powers "demon-strated."

Nothing that is genuine is used to deceive. The Holy Spirit is incapable of deception, and He can use only genuine abilities. What is used for magic is useless to Him. But what He uses cannot be used for magic. There is, however, a particular appeal in unusual abilities that can be curiously tempting. Here are strengths which the Holy Spirit wants and needs. Yet the ego sees in these same strengths an opportunity to glorify itself. Strengths turned to weakness are tragedy indeed. Yet what is not given to the Holy Spirit must be given to weakness, for what is withheld from love is given to fear, and will be fearful in consequence.

Even those who no longer value the material things of the world may still be deceived by "psychic" powers. As investment has been withdrawn from the world's material gifts, the ego has been seriously threatened. It may still be strong enough to rally under this new temptation to win back strength by guile. Many have not seen through the ego's defenses here, although they are not particularly subtle. Yet, given a remaining wish to be deceived, deception is made easy. Now the "power" is no longer a genuine ability, and cannot be used dependably. It is almost inevitable that, unless the individual changes his mind about its purpose, he will bolster his "power's" uncertainties with increasing deception.

Any ability that anyone develops has the potentiality for good. To this there is no exception. And the more unusual and unexpected the power, the greater its potential usefulness. Salvation has need of all abilities, for what the world would destroy the Holy Spirit would restore. "Psychic" abilities have been used to call upon the devil, which merely means to strengthen the ego. Yet here is also a great channel of hope and healing in the Holy Spirit's service. Those who have developed "psychic" powers have simply let some of the limitations they laid upon their minds be lifted. It can be but further limitations they lay upon themselves if they utilize their increased freedom for greater imprisonment. The Holy Spirit needs these gifts, and those who offer them to Him and Him alone go with Christ's gratitude upon their hearts, and His holy sight not far behind.

CAN GOD BE REACHED DIRECTLY?

God indeed can be reached directly, for there is no distance between Him and His Son. His awareness is in everyone's memory, and His Word is written on everyone's heart. Yet this awareness and this memory can arise across the threshold of recognition only where all barriers to truth have been removed. In how many is this the case? Here, then, is the role of God's teachers. They, too, have not attained the necessary understanding as yet, but they have joined with others. This is what sets them apart from the world. And it is this that enables others to leave the world with them. Alone they are nothing. But in their joining is the Power of God.

There are those who have reached God directly, retaining no trace of worldly limits and remembering their own Identity perfectly. These might be called the Teachers of teachers because, although they are no longer visible, their image can yet be called upon. And they will appear when and where it is helpful for them to do so. To those to whom such appearances would be frightening, they give their ideas. No one can call on them in vain. Nor is there anyone of whom they are unaware. All needs are known to them, and all mistakes are recognized and overlooked by them. The time will come when this is understood. And meanwhile, they give all their gifts to the teachers of God who look to them for help, asking all things in their Name and in no other.

Sometimes a teacher of God may have a brief experience of direct union with God. In this world, it is almost impossible that this endure. It can, perhaps, be won after much devotion and dedication, and then be maintained for much of the time on earth. But this is so rare that it cannot be considered a realistic goal. If it happens, so be it. If it does not happen, so be it as well. All worldly states must be illusory. If God were reached directly in sustained awareness, the body would not be long maintained. Those who have laid the body down merely to extend their helpfulness to those remaining behind are few indeed. And they need helpers who are still in bondage and still asleep, so that by their awakening can God's Voice be heard.

Do not despair, then, because of limitations. It is your function to escape from them, but not to be without them. If you would be heard by those who suffer, you must speak their language. If you would be a savior, you must understand what needs to be escaped. Salvation is not theoretical. Behold the problem, ask for the answer, and then accept it when it comes. Nor will its coming be long delayed. All the help you can accept will be provided, and not one need you have will not be met. Let us not, then, be too concerned with goals for which you are not ready. God takes you where you are and welcomes you. What more could you desire, when this is all you need?

WHAT IS DEATH?

Death is the central dream from which all illusions stem. Is it not madness to think of life as being born, aging, losing vitality, and dying in the end? We have asked this question before, but now we need to consider it more carefully. It is the one fixed, unchangeable belief of the world that all things in it are born only to die. This is regarded as "the way of nature," not to be raised to question, but to be accepted as the "natural" law of life. The cyclical, the changing and unsure; the undependable and the unsteady, waxing and waning in a certain way upon a certain path,—all this is taken as the Will of God. And no one asks if a benign Creator could will this.

In this perception of the universe as God created it, it would be impossible to think of Him as loving. For who has decreed that all things pass away, ending in dust and disappointment and despair, can but be feared. He holds your little life in his hand but by a thread, ready to break it off without regret or care, perhaps today. Or if he waits, yet is the ending certain. Who loves such a god knows not of love, because he has denied that life is real. Death has become life's symbol. His world is now a battleground, where contradiction reigns and opposites make endless war. Where there is death is peace impossible.

Death is the symbol of the fear of God. His Love is blotted out in the idea, which holds it from awareness like a shield held up to obscure the sun. The grimness of the symbol is enough to show it cannot coexist with God. It holds an image of the Son of God in which he is "laid to rest" in devastation's arms, where worms wait to greet him and to last a little while by his destruction. Yet the worms as well are doomed to be destroyed as certainly. And so do all things live because of death. Devouring is nature's "law of life." God is insane, and fear alone is real.

The curious belief that there is part of dying things that may go on apart from what will die, does not proclaim a loving God nor re-establish any grounds for trust. If death is real for anything, there is no life. Death denies life. But if there is reality in life, death is denied. No compromise in this is possible. There is either a god of fear or One of Love. The world attempts a thousand compromises, and will attempt a thousand more. Not one can be acceptable to God's teachers, because not one could be acceptable to God. He did not make death because He did not make fear. Both are equally meaningless to Him.

The "reality" of death is firmly rooted in the belief that God's Son is a body. And if God created bodies, death would indeed be real. But God would not be loving. There is no point at which the contrast between the perception of the real world and that of the world of illusions becomes more sharply evident. Death is indeed the death of God, if He is Love. And now His Own creation must stand in fear of Him. He is not Father, but destroyer. He is not Creator, but avenger. Terrible His Thoughts and fearful His image. To look on His creations is to die.

"And the last to be overcome will be death." Of course! Without the idea of death there is no world. All dreams will end with this one. This is salvation's final goal; the end of all illusions. And in death are all illusions born. What can be born of death and still have life? But what is born of God and still can die? The inconsistencies, the compromises and the rituals the world fosters in its vain attempts to cling to death and yet to think love real are mindless magic, ineffectual and meaningless. God is, and in Him all created things must be eternal. Do you not see that otherwise He has an opposite, and fear would be as real as love?

Teacher of God, your one assignment could be stated thus: Accept no compromise in which death plays a part. Do not believe in cruelty, nor let attack conceal the truth from you. What seems to die has but been misperceived and carried to illusion. Now it becomes your task to let the illusion be carried to the truth. Be steadfast but in this; be not deceived by the "reality" of any changing form. Truth neither moves nor wavers nor sinks down to death and dissolution. And what is the end of death? Nothing but this; the realization that the Son of God is guiltless now and forever. Nothing but this. But do not let yourself forget it is not less than this.

WHAT IS THE RESURRECTION?

Very simply, the resurrection is the overcoming or surmounting of death. It is a reawakening or a rebirth; a change of mind about the meaning of the world. It is the acceptance of the Holy Spirit's interpretation of the world's purpose; the acceptance of the Atonement for oneself. It is the end of dreams of misery, and the glad awareness of the Holy Spirit's final dream. It is the recognition of the gifts of God. It is the dream in which the body functions perfectly, having no function except communication. It is the lesson in which learning ends, for it is consummated and surpassed with this. It is the invitation to God to take His final step. It is the relinquishment of all other purposes, all other interests, all other wishes and all other concerns. It is the single desire of the Son for the Father.

The resurrection is the denial of death, being the assertion of life. Thus is all the thinking of the world reversed entirely. Life is now recognized as salvation, and pain and misery of any kind perceived as hell. Love is no longer feared, but gladly welcomed. Idols have disappeared, and the remembrance of God shines unimpeded across the world. Christ's face is seen in every living thing, and nothing is held in darkness, apart from the light of forgiveness. There is no sorrow still upon the earth. The joy of Heaven has come upon it.

Here the curriculum ends. From here on, no directions are needed. Vision is wholly corrected and all mistakes undone. Attack is meaningless and peace has come. The goal of the curriculum has been achieved. Thoughts turn to Heaven and away from hell. All longings are satisfied, for what remains unanswered or incomplete? The last illusion spreads across the world, forgiving all things and replacing all attack. The whole reversal is accomplished. Nothing is left to contradict the Word of God. There is no opposition to the truth. And now the truth can come at last. How quickly will it come as it is asked to enter and envelop such a world!

All living hearts are tranquil with a stir of deep anticipation, for the time of everlasting things is now at hand. There is no death. The Son of God is free. And in his freedom is the end of fear. No hidden places now remain on earth to shelter sick illusions, dreams of fear and misperceptions of the universe. All things are seen in light, and in the light their purpose is transformed and understood. And we, God's children, rise up from the dust and look upon our perfect sinlessness. The song of Heaven sounds around the world, as it is lifted up and brought to truth.

Now there are no distinctions. Differences have disappeared and Love looks on Itself. What further sight is needed? What remains that vision could accomplish? We have seen the face of Christ, His sinlessness, His Love behind all forms, beyond all purposes. Holy are we because His holiness has set us free indeed! And we accept His holiness as ours; as it is. As God created us so will we be forever and forever, and we wish for nothing but His Will to be our own. Illusions of another will are lost, for unity of purpose has been found.

These things await us all, but we are not prepared as yet to welcome them with joy. As long as any mind remains possessed of evil dreams, the thought of hell is real. God's teachers have the goal of wakening the minds of those asleep, and seeing there the vision of Christ's face to take the place of what they dream. The thought of murder is replaced with blessing. Judgment is laid by, and given Him Whose function judgment is. And in His final judgment is restored the truth about the holy Son of God. He is redeemed, for he has heard God's Word and understood its meaning. He is free because he let God's Voice proclaim the truth. And all he sought before to crucify are resurrected with him, by his side, as he prepares with them to meet his God.

This manual is not intended to answer all questions that both teacher and pupil may raise. In fact, it covers only a few of the more obvious ones, in terms of a brief summary of some of the major concepts in the text and workbook. It is not a substitute for either, but merely a supplement. While it is called a manual for teachers, it must be remembered that only time divides teacher and pupil, so that the difference is temporary by definition. In some cases, it may be helpful for the pupil to read the manual first. Others might do better to begin with the workbook. Still others may need to start at the more abstract level of the text.

Which is for which? Who would profit more from prayers alone? Who needs but a smile, being as yet unready for more? No one should attempt to answer these questions alone. Surely no teacher of God has come this far without realizing that. The curriculum is highly individualized, and all aspects are under the Holy Spirit's particular care and guidance. Ask and He will answer. The responsibility is His, and He alone is fit to assume it. To do so is His function. To refer the questions to Him is yours. Would you want to be responsible for decisions about which you understand so little. Be glad you have a Teacher Who cannot make a mistake. His answers are always right. Would you say that of yours?

There is another advantage,—and a very important one,—in referring decisions to the Holy Spirit with increasing frequency. Perhaps you have not thought of this aspect, but its centrality is obvious. To follow the Holy Spirit's guidance is to let yourself be absolved of guilt. It is the essence of the Atonement. It is the core of the curriculum. The imagined usurping of functions not your own is the basis of fear. The whole world you see reflects the illusion that you have done so, making fear inevitable. To return the function to the One to Whom it belongs is thus the escape from fear. And it is this that lets the memory of love return to you. Do not, then, think that following the Holy Spirit's guidance is necessary merely because of your own inadequacies. It is the way out of hell for you.

Here again is the paradox often referred to in the course. To say, "Of myself I can do nothing" is to gain all power. And yet it is but a seeming paradox. As God created you, you *have* all power. The image you made of yourself has none. The Holy Spirit knows the truth about you. The image you made does not. Yet, despite its obvious and complete ignorance, this image assumes it knows all things because you have given that belief to it. Such is your teaching, and teaching of the world that was made to uphold it. But the Teacher Who knows the truth has not forgotten it. His decisions bring benefit to all, being wholly devoid of attack. And therefore incapable of arousing guilt.

Who assumes a power that he does not possess is deceiving himself. Yet to accept the power given him by God is but to acknowledge his Creator and accept His gifts. And His gifts have no limit. To ask the Holy Spirit to decide for you is simply to accept your true inheritance. Does this mean that you cannot say anything without consulting Him? No, indeed! That would hardly be practical, and it is the practical with which this course is most concerned. If you have made it a habit to ask for help when and where you can, you can be confident that wisdom will be given you when you need it. Prepare for this each morning, remember God when you can throughout the day, ask the Holy Spirit's help when it is feasible to do so, and thank Him for His guidance at night. And your confidence will be well founded indeed.

Never forget that the Holy Spirit does not depend on your words. He understands the requests of your heart, and answers them. Does this mean that, while attack remains attractive to you, He will respond with evil? Hardly! For God has given Him the power to translate your prayers of the heart into His language. He understands that an attack is a call for help. And He responds with help accordingly. God would be cruel if He let your words replace His Own. A loving father does not let his child harm himself, or choose his own destruction. He may ask for injury, but his father will protect him still. And how much more than this does your Father love His Son?

Remember you are His completion and His Love. Remember your weakness is His strength. But do not read this hastily or wrongly. If His strength is in you, what you perceive as your weakness is but illusion. And He has given you the means to prove it so. Ask all things of His Teacher, and all things are given you. Not in the future but immediately; now. God does not wait, for waiting implies time and He is timeless. Forget your foolish images, your sense of frailty and your fear of harm, your dreams of danger and selected "wrongs." God knows but His Son, and as he was created so he is. In confidence I place you in His hands, and I give thanks for you that this is so.

And now in all your doings be you blessed.
God turns to you for help to save the world.
Teacher of God, His thanks He offers you,
And all the world stands silent in the grace
You bring from Him. You are the Son He loves,
And it is given you to be the means
Through which His Voice is heard around the world,
To close all things of time; to end the sight
Of all things visible; and to undo
All things that change. Through you is ushered in
A world unseen, unheard, yet truly there.
Holy are you, and in your light the world
Reflects your holiness, for you are not
Alone and friendless. I give thanks for you,
And join your efforts on behalf of God,
Knowing they are on my behalf as well,
And for all those who walk to God with me.

AMEN

CLARIFICATION OF TERMS

INTRODUCTION

This is not a course in philosophical speculation, nor is it concerned with precise terminology. It is concerned only with Atonement, or the correction of perception. The means of the Atonement is forgiveness. The structure of "individual consciousness" is essentially irrelevant because it is a concept representing the "original error" or the "original sin." To study the error itself does not lead to correction, if you are indeed to succeed in overlooking the error. And it is just this process of overlooking at which the course aims.

All terms are potentially controversial, and those who seek controversy will find it. Yet those who seek clarification will find it as well. They must, however, be willing to overlook controversy, recognizing that it is a defense against truth in the form of a delaying maneuver. Theological considerations as such are necessarily controversial, since they depend on belief and can therefore be accepted or rejected. A universal theology is impossible, but a universal experience is not only possible but necessary. It is this experience toward which the course is directed. Here alone consistency becomes possible because here alone uncertainty ends.

This course remains within the ego framework, where it is needed. It is not concerned with what is beyond all error because it is planned only to set the direction towards it. Therefore it uses words, which are symbolic, and cannot express what lies beyond symbols. It is merely the ego that questions because it is only the ego that doubts. The course merely gives another answer, once a question has been raised. However, this answer does not attempt to resort to inventiveness or ingenuity. These are attributes of the ego. *The course is simple*. It has one function and one goal. Only in that does it remain wholly consistent because only that can *be* consistent.

The ego will demand many answers that this course does not give. It does not recognize as questions the mere form of a question to which an answer is impossible. The ego may ask, "How did the impossible occur?", "To what did the impossible happen?", and may ask this in many forms. Yet there is no answer; only an experience. Seek only this, and do not let theology delay you.

You will notice that the emphasis on structural issues in the course is brief and early. Afterwards and soon, it drops away to make way for the central teaching. Since you have asked for clarification, however, these are some of the terms that are used.

MIND — SPIRIT

The term *mind* is used to represent the activating agent of spirit, supplying its creative energy. When the term is capitalized it refers to God or Christ (i.e., the Mind of God or the Mind of Christ). *Spirit* is the Thought of God which He created like Himself. The unified spirit is God's one Son, or Christ.

In this world, because the mind is split, the Sons of God appear to be separate. Nor do their minds seem to be joined. In this illusory state, the concept of an "individual mind" seems to be meaningful. It is therefore described in the course *as if* it has two parts; spirit and ego.

Spirit is the part that is still in contact with God through the Holy Spirit, Who abides in this part but sees the other part as well. The term "soul" is not used except in direct Biblical quotations because of its highly controversial nature. It would, however, be an equivalent of "spirit," with the understanding that, being of God, it is eternal and was never born.

The other part of the mind is entirely illusory and makes only illusions. Spirit retains the potential for creating, but its Will, which is God's, seems to be imprisoned while the mind is not unified. Creation continues unabated because that is the Will of God. This Will is always unified and therefore has no meaning in this world. It has no opposite and no degrees.

The mind can be right or wrong, depending on the voice to which it listens. *Right-mindedness* listens to the Holy Spirit, forgives the world, and through Christ's vision sees the real world in its place. This is the final vision, the last perception, the condition in which God takes the final step Himself. Here time and illusions end together.

Wrong-mindedness listens to the ego and makes illusions; perceiving sin and justifying anger, and seeing guilt, disease and death as real. Both this world and the real world are illusions because right-mindedness merely overlooks, or forgives, what never happened. Therefore it is not the *One-mindedness* of the Christ Mind, Whose Will is one with God's.

In this world the only remaining freedom is the freedom of choice; always between two choices or two voices. Will is not involved in perception at any level, and has nothing to do with choice. *Consciousness* is the receptive mechanism, receiving messages from above or below; from the Holy Spirit or the ego

Consciousness has levels and awareness can shift quite dramatically, but it cannot transcend the perceptual realm. At its highest it becomes aware of the real world, and can be trained to do so increasingly. Yet the very fact that it has levels and can be trained demonstrates that it cannot reach knowledge.

THE EGO — THE MIRACLE

Illusions will not last. Their death is sure and this alone is certain in their world. It is the ego's world because of this. What is the *ego*? But a dream of what you really are. A thought you are apart from your Creator and a wish to be what He created not. It is a thing of madness, not reality at all. A name for namelessness is all it is. A symbol of impossibility; a choice for options that do not exist. We name it but to help us understand that it is nothing but an ancient thought that what is made has immortality. But what could come of this except a dream which, like all dreams, can only end in death?

What is the ego? Nothingness, but in a form that seems like something. In a world of form the ego cannot be denied for it alone seems real. Yet could God's Son as He created him abide in form or in a world of form? Who asks you to define the ego and explain how it arose can be but he who thinks it real, and seeks by definition to ensure that its illusive nature is concealed behind the words that seem to make it so.

There is no definition for a lie that serves to make it true. Nor can there be a truth that lies conceal effectively. The ego's unreality is not denied by words nor is its meaning clear because its nature seems to have a form. Who can define the undefinable? And yet there is an answer even here.

We cannot make a definition for what the ego is, but we *can* say what it is not. And this is shown to us with perfect clarity. It is from this that we deduce all that the ego is. Look at its opposite and you can see the only answer that is meaningful.

The ego's opposite in every way,—in origin, effect and consequence — we call a miracle. And here we find all that is not the ego in this world. Here is the ego's opposite and here alone we look on what the ego was, for here we see all that it seemed to do, and cause and its effects must still be one.

Where there was darkness now we see the light. What is the ego? What the darkness was. Where is the ego? Where the darkness was. What is it now and where can it be found? Nothing and nowhere. Now the light has come: its opposite has gone without a trace. Where evil was there now is holiness. What is the ego? What the evil was. Where is the ego? In an evil dream that but seemed real while you were dreaming it. Where there was crucifixion stands God's Son. What is the ego? Who has need to ask? Where is the ego? Who has the need to seek for an illusion now that dreams are gone?

What is a *miracle*? A dream as well. But look at all the aspects of *this* dream and you will never question any more. Look at the kindly world you see extend before you as you walk in gentleness. Look at the helpers all along the way you travel, happy in the certainty of Heaven and the surety of peace. And look an instant, too, on what you left behind at last and finally passed by.

This was the ego — all the cruel hate, the need for vengeance and the cries of pain, the fear of dying and the urge to kill, the brotherless illusion and the self that seemed alone in all the universe. This terrible mistake about yourself the miracle corrects as gently as a loving mother sings her child to rest. Is not a song like this what you would hear? Would it not answer all you thought to ask, and even make the question meaningless?

Your questions have no answer, being made to still God's Voice, Which asks of everyone one question only: "Are you ready yet to help Me save the world?" Ask this instead of what the ego is, and you will see a sudden brightness cover up the world the ego made. No miracle is now withheld from anyone. The world is saved from what you thought it was. And what it is, is wholly uncondemned and wholly pure.

The miracle forgives; the ego damns. Neither need be defined except by this. Yet could a definition be more sure, or more in line with what salvation is? Problem and answer lie together here, and having met at last the choice is clear. Who chooses hell when it is recognized? And who would not go on a little while when it is given him to understand the way is short and Heaven is his goal?

FORGIVENESS — THE FACE OF CHRIST

Forgiveness is for God and toward God but not of Him. It is impossible to think of anything He created that could need forgiveness. Forgiveness, then, is an illusion, but because of its purpose, which is the Holy Spirit's, it has one difference. Unlike all other illusions it leads away from error and not towards it.

Forgiveness might be called a kind of happy fiction; a way in which the unknowing can bridge the gap between their perception and the truth. They cannot go directly from perception to knowledge because they do not think it is their will to do so. This makes God appear to be an enemy instead of what He really is. And it is just this insane perception that makes them unwilling merely to rise up and to return to Him in peace.

And so they need an illusion of help because they are helpless; a Thought of peace because they are in conflict. God knows what His Son needs before he asks. He is not at all concerned with form, but having given the content it is His Will that it be understood. And that suffices. The form adapts itself to need; the content is unchanging, as eternal as its Creator.

The face of Christ has to be seen before the memory of God can return. The reason is obvious. Seeing the face of Christ involves perception. No one can look on knowledge. But the face of Christ is the great symbol of forgiveness. It is salvation. It is the symbol of the real world. Whoever looks on this no longer sees the world. He is as near to Heaven as is possible outside the gate. Yet from this gate it is no more than just a step inside. It is the final step. And this we leave to God.

Forgiveness is a symbol, too, but as the symbol of His Will alone it cannot be divided. And so the Unity that it reflects becomes His Will. It is the only thing still in the world in part, and yet the bridge to Heaven.

God's Will is all there is. We can but go from nothingness to everything; from hell to Heaven. Is this a journey? No, not in truth, for truth goes nowhere. But illusions shift from place to place; from time to time. The final step is also but a shift. As a perception it is part unreal. And yet this part will vanish. What remains is peace eternal and the Will of God.

There are no wishes now for wishes change. Even the wished-for can become unwelcome. That must be so because the ego cannot be at peace. But Will is constant, as the gift of God. And what He gives is always like Himself. This is the purpose of the face of Christ. It is the gift of God to save His Son. But look on this and you have been forgiven.

How lovely does the world become in just that single instant when you see the truth about yourself reflected there. Now you are sinless and behold your sinlessness. Now you are holy and perceive it so. And now the mind returns to its Creator; the joining of the Father and the Son, the Unity of unities that stands behind all joining but beyond them all. God is not seen but only understood. His Son is not attacked but recognized.

The world you see is an illusion of a world. God did not creace it, for what He creates must be eternal as Himself. Yet there is nothing in the world you see that will endure forever. Some things will last in time a little while longer than others. But the time will come when all things visible will have an end.

The body's eyes are therefore not the means by which the real world can be seen, for the illusions that they look upon must lead to more illusions of reality. And so they do. For everything they see not only will not last, but lends itself to thoughts of sin and guilt. While everything that God created is forever without sin and therefore is forever without guilt.

Knowledge is not the remedy for false perception since, being another level, they can never meet. The one correction possible for false perception must be *true perception.* It will not endure. But for the time it lasts it comes to heal. For true perception is a remedy with many names. Forgiveness, salvation, Atonement, true perception, all are one. They are the one beginning, with the end to lead to Oneness far beyond themselves. True perception is the means by which the world is saved from sin, for sin does not exist. And it is this that true perception sees.

The world stands like a block before Christ's face. But true perception looks on it as nothing more than just a fragile veil, so easily dispelled that it can last no longer than an instant. It is seen at last for only what it is. And now it cannot fail to disappear, for now there is an empty place made clean and ready. Where destruction was perceived the face of Christ appears, and in that instant is the world forgot, with time forever ended as the world spins into nothingness from where it came.

A world forgiven cannot last. It was the home of bodies. But forgiveness looks past bodies. This is its holiness; this is how it heals. The world of bodies is the world of sin, for only if there were a body is sin possible. From sin comes guilt as surely as forgiveness takes all guilt away. And once all guilt is gone what more remains to keep a separated world in place? For place has gone as well, along with time. Only the body makes the world seem real, for being separate it could not remain where separation is impossible. Forgiveness proves it is impossible because it sees it not. And what you then will overlook will not be understandable to you, just as its presence once had been your certainty.

This is the shift that true perception brings: What was projected out is seen within, and there forgiveness lets it disappear. For there the altar to the Son is set, and there his Father is remembered. Here are all illusions brought to truth and laid upon the altar. What is seen outside must lie beyond forgiveness, for it seems to be forever sinful. Where is hope while sin is seen as outside? What remedy can guilt expect? But seen within your mind, guilt and forgiveness for an instant lie together, side by side, upon one altar. There at last are sickness and its single remedy joined in one healing brightness. God has come to claim His Own. Forgiveness is complete.

And now God's *knowledge*, changeless, certain, pure and wholly understandable, enters its kingdom. Gone is perception, false and true alike. Gone is forgiveness, for its task is done. And gone are bodies in the blazing light upon the altar to the Son of God. God knows it is His Own, as it is his. And here they join, for here the face of Christ has shone away time's final instant, and now is the last perception of the world without a purpose and without a cause. For where God's memory has come at last there is no journey, no belief in sin, no walls, no bodies, and the grim appeal of guilt and death is there snuffed out forever.

O my brothers, if you only knew the peace that will envelop you and hold you safe and pure and lovely in the Mind of God, you could but rush to meet Him where His altar is. Hallowed your name and His, for they are joined here in this holy place. Here He leans down to lift you up to Him, out of illusions into holiness; out of the world and to eternity; out of all fear and given back to love.

There is no need for help to enter Heaven for you have never left. But there is need for help beyond yourself as you are circumscribed by false beliefs of your Identity, Which God alone established in reality. Helpers are given you in many forms, although upon the altar they are one. Beyond each one there is a Thought of God, and this will never change. But they have names which differ for a time, for time needs symbols, being itself unreal. Their names are legion, but we will not go beyond the names the course itself employs. God does not help because He knows no need. But He creates all Helpers of His Son while he believes his fantasies are true. Thank God for them for they will lead you home.

The name of *Jesus* is the name of one who was a man but saw the face of Christ in all his brothers and remembered God. So he became identified with *Christ*, a man no longer, but at one with God. The man was an illusion, for he seemed to be a separate being, walking by himself, within a body that appeared to hold his self from Self, as all illusions do. Yet who can save unless he sees illusions and then identifies them as what they are? Jesus remains a Savior because he saw the false without accepting it as true. And Christ needed his form that He might appear to men and save them from their own illusions.

In his complete identification with the Christ — the perfect Son of God, His one creation and His happiness, forever like Himself and one with Him — Jesus became what all of you must be. He led the way for you to follow him. He leads you back to God because he saw the road before him, and he followed it. He made a clear distinction, still obscure to you, between the false and true. He offered you a final demonstration that it is impossible to kill God's Son; nor can his life in any way be changed by sin and evil, malice, fear or death.

And therefore all your sins have been forgiven because they carried no effects at all. And so they were but dreams. Arise with him who showed you this because you owe him this who shared your dreams that they might be dispelled. And shares them still, to be at one with you.

Is he the Christ? O yes, along with you. His little life on earth was not enough to teach the mighty lesson that he learned for all of you. He will remain with you to lead you from the hell you made to God. And when you join your will with his, your sight will be his vision, for the eyes of Christ are shared. Walking with him is just as natural as walking with a brother whom you knew since you were born, for such indeed he is. Some bitter idols have been made of him who would be only brother to the world. Forgive him your illusions, and behold how dear a brother he would be to you. For he will set your mind at rest at last and carry it with you unto your God.

Is he God's only Helper? No, indeed. For Christ takes many forms with different names until their oneness can be recognized. But Jesus is for you the bearer of Christ's single message of the Love of God. You need no other. It is possible to read his words and benefit from them without accepting him into your life. Yet he would help you yet a little more if you will share your pains and joys with him, and leave them both to find the peace of God. Yet still it is his lesson most of all that he would have you learn, and it is this:

> *"There is no death because the Son of God is like his Father. Nothing you can do can change Eternal Love. Forget your dreams of sin and guilt, and come with me instead to share the resurrection of God's Son. And bring with you all those whom He has sent to you to care for as I care for you."*

THE HOLY SPIRIT

Jesus is the manifestation of the *Holy Spirit*, Whom he called down upon the earth after he ascended into Heaven, or became completely identified with the Christ, the Son of God as He created him. The Holy Spirit, being a creation of the One Creator, creating with Him and in His likeness or spirit, is eternal and has never changed. He was "called down upon the earth" in the sense that it was now possible to accept Him and to hear His Voice. His is the Voice for God, and has therefore taken form. This form is not His reality, which God alone knows along with Christ, His real Son, Who is part of Him.

The Holy Spirit is described throughout the course as giving us the answer to the separation and bringing the plan of the Atonement to us, establishing our particular part in it and showing us exactly what it is. He has established Jesus as the leader in carrying out His plan since he was the first to complete his own part perfectly. All power in Heaven and earth is therefore given him and he will share it with you when you have completed yours. The Atonement principle was given to the Holy Spirit long before Jesus set it in motion.

The Holy Spirit is described as the remaining communication link between God and His separated Sons. In order to fulfill this special function the Holy Spirit has assumed a dual function. He knows because He is part of God; He perceives because He was sent to save humanity. He is the great correction principle; the bringer of true perception, the inherent power of the vision of Christ. He is the light in which the forgiven world is perceived; in which the face of Christ alone is seen. He never forgets the Creator or His Creation. He never forgets the Son of God. He never forgets you. And He brings the Love of your Father to you in an eternal shining that will never be obliterated because God has put it there.

The Holy Spirit abides in the part of your mind that is part of the Christ Mind. He represents your Self and your Creator, Who are one. He speaks for God and also for you, being joined with both. And therefore it is He Who proves them one. He seems to be a Voice, for in that form He speaks God's Word to you. He seems to be a Guide through a far country, for you need that form of help. He seems to be whatever meets the needs you think you have. But He is not deceived when you perceive your self entrapped in needs you do not have. It is from these He would deliver you. It is fron these that He would make you safe.

You are His manifestation in this world. Your brother calls to you to be His Voice along with him. Alone he cannot be the Helper of God's Son for he alone is functionless. But joined with you he is the shining Savior of the world, Whose part in its redemption you have made complete. He offers thanks to you as well as him for you arose with him when he began to save the world. And you will be with him when time is over and no trace remains of dreams of spite in which you dance to death's thin melody. For in its place the hymn to God is heard a little while. And then the Voice is gone, no longer to take form but to return to the eternal Formlessness of God.

Forget not once this journey is begun the end is certain. Doubt along the way will come and go and go to come again. Yet is the ending sure. No one can fail to do what God appointed him to do. When you forget, remember that you walk with Him and with His Word upon your heart. Who could despair when Hope like this is his? Illusions of despair may seem to come, but learn how not to be deceived by them. Behind each one there is reality and there is God. Why would you wait for this and trade it for illusions, when His Love is but an instant farther on the road where all illusions end? The end *is* sure and guaranteed by God. Who stands before a lifeless image when a step away the Holy of the Holies opens up an ancient door that leads beyond the world?

You *are* a stranger here. But you belong to Him Who loves you as He loves Himself. Ask but my help to roll the stone away, and it is done according to His Will. We *have* begun the journey. Long ago the end was written in the stars and set into the Heavens with a shining ray that held it safe within eternity and through all time as well. And holds it still; unchanged, unchanging and unchangeable.

Be not afraid. We only start again an ancient journey long ago begun that but seems new. We have begun again upon a road we travelled on before and lost our way a little while. And now we try again. Our new beginning has the certainty the journey lacked till now. Look up and see His Word among the stars, where He has set your name along with His. Look up and find your certain destiny the world would hide but God would have you see.

Let us wait here in silence, and kneel down an instant in our gratitude to Him Who called to us and helped us hear His Call. And then let us arise and go in faith along the way to Him. Now we are sure we do not walk alone. For God is here, and with Him all our brothers. Now we know that we will never lose the way again. The song begins again which had been stopped only an instant, though it seems to be unsung forever. What is here begun will grow in life and strength and hope, until the world is still an instant and forgets all that the dream of sin had made of it.

Let us go out and meet the newborn world, knowing that Christ has been reborn in it, and that the holiness of this rebirth will last forever. We had lost our way but He has found it for us. Let us go and bid Him welcome Who returns to us to celebrate salvation and the end of all we thought we made. The morning star of this new day looks on a different world where God is welcomed and His Son with Him. We who complete Him offer thanks to Him, as He gives thanks to us. The Son is still, and in the quiet God has given him enters his home and is at peace at last.